'To dream of being in tears and then to actually wake up and discover we are actually crying, suggests that some hurt or trauma has come sufficiently close to the surface to enable us to deal with it on a conscious level.'

Pamela Ball, 1990

Dr. Crank & Staff

April 2013

This book is dedicated with thanks to my husband Neil,
Our children, Graham, Hazel and Geoffrey
The road I've travelled has been long and difficult,
But you've held my hand and wiped my tears.
As a family we are bound together by an
invisible thread
Of love, compassion and kindness.

SILENT NO MORE

Dee Arm

First published in 2012
Reprinted April 2013

ISBN: 978-1-62407-620-6

Printed by
Nightingale Press Ltd
Newark Close
Royston
Hertfordshire
SG8 5HL

Special thanks to Vivian Foster of Bookscribe, your help and guidance has been invaluable.

Time passes, wounds heal and
silent tears still fall.

Doreen Daisy
1935-2000

Hope includes a shared story
Hope includes stories of a meaning
Hope includes an affirmative story
Hope includes the real story

CONTENTS

Special Thanks . . . 8

Author's Note . . . 9

Prologue . . . 12

CHAPTER ONE:

One Day in My Life . . . 15

CHAPTER TWO:

The Diaries . . . 18

CHAPTER THREE:

Trying to Understand . . . 28

CHAPTER FOUR:

A Little Bit of History . . . 33

CHAPTER FIVE:

On Reflection . . . 38

CHAPTER SIX:

Progression . . . 41

CHAPTER SEVEN:

The Family is Growing . . . 49

CHAPTER EIGHT:

Good Times, Bad Times . . . 56

CHAPTER NINE:

Returning Home . . . 93

CHAPTER TEN:

All About Mother . . . 95

CHAPTER ELEVEN:

1978. 110

CHAPTER TWELVE:

Together We Are Beautiful.. 115

CHAPTER THIRTEEN:

More About Father.. 130

CHAPTER FOURTEEN:

Finding Out About The Adopted Twins 140

CHAPTER FIFTEEN:

Mum's Death (2000).. 147

CHAPTER SIXTEEN:

Charity Parachute Jump for Ali. 152

CHAPTER SEVENTEEN:

Careers Are For Men, Not Women 157

CHAPTER EIGHTEEN:

Grenada and My Empty Nest Syndrome 166

CHAPTER NINETEEN:

What Happened in Jersey?.. 184

CHAPTER TWENTY:

The Most Perfect Day 187

CHAPTER TWENTY-ONE:

The Year 2011 190

CHAPTER TWENTY-TWO:

The Road to Recovery and What's in a Dream?.. 196

CHAPTER TWENTY-THREE: A Little About Me 263

A message from Neil. 271

References.. 272

Special Thanks

Firstly, I would like to thank my husband and best friend, Neil. He has been at my side during the happiest and darkest moments of my life over the last thirty-three years. Without his continuous love, encouragement and support this book would still be unwritten. Without him beside me, holding my hand I would have been lost forever.

I would also like to thank my very special counsellor Helen. She is a truly unique individual with all the special qualities, skills and intuitive nature that make an amazing counsellor. Helen, over a two and a half year period helped me to understand my inner turmoil. Working together, she has enabled me to unlock my traumatic childhood, to understand it and become the person I am today.

Also, special thanks to Diane, who herself has struggled with her own traumas of abuse from early childhood. Diane has always been there for me. There are no words in the English dictionary that describe the unconditional love that I have for such a special courageous woman. I am truly blessed to have her as my sister. In her own words, 'she is always behind me'.

I would also like to thank my sister Mandy. Your words of encouragement helped me to believe in myself and tell my story. Without your inspiration, motivation and precious time so freely given, this book would still be a draft copy. You are one in a million and I thank you from the bottom of my heart.

There are many others who have touched my life along the way in some form or another, those of you will know who you are and I am forever thankful.

Author's Note

The story I have told in this book is autobiographical. Along with the sadness and pain that I have experienced during my life, there have also been profound moments of enlightenment and joy. I have used italics to indicate dreams, flashbacks and nightmares so please keep this in mind when reading this book.

Any references to the numerals 150 and 56 are the numbers of the first two houses that I lived in as a child growing up.

After countless months of researching, I have gained access to my late mother's general practitioner notes, hospital mental health records and other important documents. These records for the first time in my life have enabled me to build an accurate timeline of some events that were lost to my memory. These were events that took place during my early years, ones that I only had vague recollections of, but were aware had happened. Now, at last, I have a true, factual picture and a better understanding of the decline of my mother's health and my own childhood. All the information in this book to the best of my knowledge is accurate.

My brothers and sisters will have their own accounts of their upbringing and childhood memories. I have given my siblings an open invitation to view the book before publication and some have taken the opportunity to do this while others have not. I have also changed some names to protect their identities.

Below is my family tree which I hope will enable readers to identify the individuals mentioned on the following pages. Covered in the book are some of my earliest memories to the present day. It is the true story of how I have come to terms with an unbelievable, lost and tragic childhood and survived.

Also covered in this book are some true events told to me by my sister Diane, and who has given her permission for them to be included. This is the true story of a dysfunctional, horrendous household run by a sadistic, evil and very clever man – my father.

My beautiful mother untouched by my father

Mother
Doreen Daisy Nott

Father
Geoffrey George Arm

1957	1958	1959	1960	1961	1963	1968	1969	1971	1972	1974
Sharon	Simon	**Denise**	Diane Kevin	Sue Steve (*adopted*)	Mandy Wendy	Sarah	Sandra	Lawrence	Penny	Adam

Originally, the dreams, nightmares and flashbacks that I experienced were not intended to be included in the book. They were simply written as a personal journal in 2007–2010 to be used as part of my own recovery process from the trauma of my childhood abuse. Many of my dreams, I believe, have a direct link to my past and for this reason I believe it is paramount that these are all included. Working with the dreams through counselling and therapy, I have been able to unlock my early years. I have now come to terms with the loss and am able to understand the feelings of detachment, frustration, sadness, anger and sense of loneliness that have haunted my waking hours. Writing this book has been one of the most significant steps that I have made towards my own recovery. If this in turn inspires one other person to follow in my footsteps to seek help and to keep a dream journal/diary, then it has all been worthwhile.

Prologue

I shouldn't have written this book ... but I have.
I shouldn't be telling this story ... but I am.
You shouldn't be reading this ... but you are.

And so my story begins… Once upon a time there lived a family of skeletons.

The family of skeletons are hiding in the dark abyss at the back of a closet. The year is 1980 and the time has come for them to venture out from their hiding place into the light. One by one they emerge, each one carrying a piece of a jigsaw puzzle. I am not a skeleton; I am the gate keeper. I have collected the pieces from each skeleton over many years and they are, oh, so heavy. I must place them down on a table and spread them out for all to see. There are so many pieces both large and small, that it is hard to find room for them all. Finally, slowly and with methodical accuracy I can start to piece them together.

The worn out jigsaw is gradually coming to life. The picture the pieces portray is grim and what begins to emerge is that my family are living in a dysfunctional, horrendous household, run by an evil, sadistic man – my father.

My mother knew all the secrets of the skeletons concealed within the closet. She held copies of each piece of the jigsaw deep within her psychotic mind. She would hold these pieces for her entire lifetime and carry their secrets to her grave. She was trapped in a world of voices, physical abuse and mental torture from the moment she met my father. The man she fell in love with held her life in his hands as if he owned her very soul. Mother was delicate, beautiful and innocent, like a newly-hatched butterfly trapped in a jar. I could see her, but I would never be able to reach her, however hard I tried. There would be no escape for my mother, because my father held the jar in his evil hands with the lid tightly shut.

I was born into this dysfunctional family in 1959 and during the next thirty years I would witness and experience things that would shape my life for ever. My healing and recovery will take a lifetime and I too will carry the pieces of the jigsaw to my grave. But for me there is a difference; unlike my virtually silent, mute mother I have found my voice. A voice that is powerful as my conscience is now clear and my soul is on a journey to freedom. I have escaped from the confines of that jar.

Now, as memories, flashbacks and dreams slowly rear their ugly heads I can begin to see my past for what it was. The year I start my story is 1980.

HOPES AND DREAMS

Hope is the thing with feathers
That perches in the soul...
And sings the tune without words
And never stops ... at all

Emily Dickinson (1861)

CHAPTER ONE

One Day in My Life

I hear the familiar sound of the front door closing – am I asleep or awake? I'm not sure! I hear footsteps coming up the stairs and the click of knees as they make each step – it is such a haunting sound. I know you are there, all my senses are awake. My heart is pounding in my chest so fast and loud, I am sure you can hear it. I'm lying still in the bed unable to move, not daring to breathe. Locked in a lucid dream! A flashback! 'Keep still, don't move,' I tell myself. Then the covers move slightly, a little tug, a silent pull. The weight of you makes the bed sink. I feel your hands touching me, then you are on top of me moving. How do I know what is going on, for I am just a baby, a toddler, a child … with my eyes tightly shut.

I am awake and crying, trying to make sense yet again of the moment that has just passed. I can feel my heart pounding in my chest and there is a nauseating feeling deep in the pit of my stomach. It is Saturday morning, my husband has already left for work and I am lying in bed in our beautiful bedroom. The sun streams through a gap in the curtain and dances on the wall. I am twenty-one years old. I am confused, frightened and feeling very alone. I say to myself, 'pull yourself together, you're ok. It was just a dream'. But how can it be just a dream? It was so real! At the time I had no idea why I should be having such a horrific dream/flashback. How dare this happen to me and intrude into my world of newly-wedded bliss.

After an initial assessment in 2006 and having to wait until the following year, I was fortunate enough to work with a remarkable lady named Helen. Helen works as a volunteer counsellor for an organisation called Choices which is based in Cambridge. It specialises in working with both male and female adults who have survived the trauma of sexual abuse. Without her support, kindness and knowledge, I believe I would not be here writing this today. The healing process takes many different stages and for me continues to this day. Writing this book has been a roller coaster of emotions. There have been days when I have sat down to write, only to open the page and then close it again within seconds. It has taken a tremendous amount of courage, commitment and pain to put pen to paper. I have always had a little voice inside me saying, 'write it down … speak the truth … you have nothing to hide'. I am not afraid of the truth anymore as I have faced my demons head on, unlike some unfortunate people. There have been ups and downs, tears of laughter and far too many tears of sorrow, but today I can hold my head up high and bravely smile at people day in and day out. My tears will still come at the most inappropriate times but now at last, I can allow them to fall.

C. S. Lewis wrote about the bottle of child's tears that heals any wound with just one drop. Tears in myths, melt the icy heart. In the Inuit story *The Stone Child* by Dan Poblocki, a boy's hot tears cause a cold stone to break open, releasing a protective spirit. In the tale, *Mary Culhane,* the demon who has seized Mary cannot enter any house where there are tears cried by a true heart; these he considers 'holy water'.

Clarissa Pinkola Estès wrote in *Women Who Run With The Wolves*: 'All through history, tears have done three works;

called the spirits to one's side, repelled those who would muffle and bind the simple soul, and healed the injuries of poor human bargains.'

'There are times in a woman's life when she cries and cries and cries and even though she has the succour and support of her loved ones, still and yet she cries. Something in this crying keeps the predator away, keeps away unhealthy desire or gain that will ruin her. Tears are part of the mending of rips in the psyche where energy has leaked and leaked away. The matter is serious, but the worst does not occur – our light is not stolen – for tears make us conscious. There is no chance to go back to sleep when one is weeping. Whatever sleep comes is then "only rest for the physical body".'

'Sometimes a woman says, "I am sick of crying, I am tired of it, I want it to stop." But it is her soul that is making the tears, and they are her protection. So she must keep on till of need is over. Some women marvel at all the water their bodies can produce when they weep. It will not last forever, only till the soul is done with its wise expression.'

As I read the above I am filled with such emotion and a connection with all silent abuse victims. Today I am reminded of my own transformation.

CHAPTER TWO

The Diaries

If something is unmentionable,
it is also unmanageable.
Folk Wisdom

I have managed to keep diaries since my early teens; they are full of useful and useless information about my life to date. Although I found it easy to put words onto the pages of my diary, there have been many times since that I have struggled to read those words, words that open up old wounds. As an adult I am so glad that I took the time to record these events and feelings because I know they would otherwise have been forgotten and lost forever. During my two-and-a-half years of counselling with Choices I wrote a separate journal of all the dreams, flashbacks and nightmares that I have experienced. Interpreting these dreams has helped me to understand and unlock the trauma that I had to experience every day for many of my early years. Later in this book there is a separate section of all the dreams I had during that time. They are logged in chronological order and I believe hold the key to some events early in my childhood.

Dear Diary

Monday, July 15th 1974

Today I got a kitten and I have named it Tinker. He is ten weeks old and ginger. Already house trained. Number 1 in the charts *She*.

Wednesday, July 17th 1974

I cooked a dinner of beef burgers, carrots and potato. Dad did not come home lunchtime. Mum was slamming things down again. Dad had a bad stomach. I cooked dad's dinner.

Saturday, July 20th 1974

Working at Bartons the bakers.

Tuesday, July 23rd 1974

Bought myself a ring, it has green stones in it. One fell out so I took one from mum's necklace.

Thursday, 25th July 1974

Dad said I fancied Alan and that he didn't want any divorced people in our house.

Friday, July 26th 1974

Dad gave me 50p for tomorrow's dinner. Won't work Monday will be looking after little ones.

Sunday, July 28th 1974

Kim's dad hit her; I didn't think he was like that. She has to stay in for the rest of the holidays.

Thursday, August 1st 1974
Dad told me and Simon off and now we have to tidy the house. Dad annoyed again. Aunty Lily said she feels sorry for us.

Friday, August 2nd 1974
Lily took mum out.

Saturday, August 3rd 1974
Lily took mum out again. Dad annoyed again; he bought paints. Mum smashed the window.

Monday, August 5th 1974
Sharon and Derek took me to Woburn Abbey. I had a lovely day looking at the lions, tigers and the monkeys climbing on the car.

Tuesday, August 6th 1974
Dad annoyed again, told me not to talk to Alan.

Thursday, August 8th 1974
Dad spoke to Alan I was very upset. Alan is twenty-five and I'm fifteen.

Friday, August 9th 1974
Dad told me off again I had no dinner and went back out.

Sunday, August 11th 1974
Cost 17p to get into Stanborough swimming pool. Borrowed a cossie from Hilary.

Monday, August 19th 1974
Staying at Aunty Betty's house. Lily's house first.

Thursday, August 22nd 1974
Went to Enfield town with Dawn and Jane and had our photo done. We played badminton. Aunty Betty gave me some clothes.

Tuesday, August 27th 1974
I collected the family allowance and did the shopping. Tracey's dog stinks, flipping thing.

Thursday, August 29th 1974
Dad said we might be moving I don't want to move.
Went to Hatfield with Diane to look for a skirt.

Monday, September 2nd 1974
Simon started work. I need to get stuff for school.

Tuesday, September 3rd 1974
Back to school, oh god! Wore Sharon's shoes and they were too small.

Saturday, April 10th 1976
I said mum looked really nice. Mum and Dad away to Portsmouth for Nan and Granddad's golden wedding anniversary.

Tuesday, September 14th 1976
The telephone has been disconnected.

Tuesday, October 5th 1976
Diane went to get mums tablets from the surgery. Mum's not very well today and she frightened me.

Friday, November 5th 1976
Dad said he was having trouble with a lady from work, she kept phoning him up.

Monday, February 28th 1977
Dad has gone to Blackpool.

Friday, April 1st 1977
I had written mum had been ill for seven years. I was also worried because she had been losing a lot of blood.

Wednesday, April 6th 1977
Took little ones for a walk to the chalk pits.

Thursday, April 7th 1977
Dad's in a bad mood again.

Friday, April 15th 1977
Mandy has a swollen face, Diane large tonsils and Wendy going the same way.

Sunday, April 17th 1977
Took Penny and Lawrence to Jean's house home for 7.30.

Monday, April 18th 1977
Dressed Lawrence. Dad's annoyed about Simon's bedroom. I went to Stevenage on the train and bought three tops for summer.

Wednesday, April 20th 1977
Gave Wendy my socks.

Thursday, April 21st 1977
£15 deposit for bike from Halfords.

Tuesday, April 26th 1977
Me German measles.

Friday, April 29th 1977
Dad going to Billingham.

Saturday, May 7th 1977
Dad got motorbike 550cc black Honda.

Monday, September 12th 1977
Started new job at the hospital and I like it.

Friday, April 7th 1978
Sandra and Diane away with Iris.

Saturday, April 8th 1978
Dad in a foul mood. I cooked dinner and did the housework.

Friday, June 16th 1978
Dad stayed at Harry's last night.

Monday, June 19th 1978
Mum back into hospital. Iris took her.

Tuesday, June 20th 1978
Mum is sixteen weeks pregnant. Termination on Thursday and Sharon sent flowers.

Wednesday, June 21st 1978
I was upset. Saw mum on Codicote ward.

Sunday, June 25th 1978
Went to visit mum with dad.

Monday, June 26th 1978
Visit mum at lunchtime.

Wednesday, June 28th 1978
Mum still in hospital.

Thursday, June 29th 1978
Mum did not look well. Children all going away Friday for the weekend.

Friday, June 30th 1978
Harry and Tracey came round. Went to see mum again.

Tuesday, July 4th 1978
Love my family. Mum seems to be improving and coping. The children are fine.

Tuesday, July 11th 1978
Visited mum during my lunch hour.

Thursday, July 13th 1978
Visited mum, Sharon also visited.

Saturday, July 15th 1978
Mum home for the weekend.

Sunday, July 16th 1978
Sunday dad really annoyed mum, she kicked up quite a fuss about going back into hospital

Monday, July 17th 1978
Mum seemed ok.

Tuesday, July 18th 1978
Stayed after work to see mum

Friday, July 21st 1978
Mum home today.

Sunday, July 23rd 1978
Dad's having an affair with Tracey so he is ok.

Tuesday, July 25th 1978
Mum is shouting and swearing

Thursday, July 27th 1978
Man from the hospital came to visit mum.

Friday, July 28th 1978
Iris lent me a red vanity case it is lovely. Dad's up to something.

Saturday, November 18th 1978
Dad has gone to Jersey again.

Saturday, April 7th 1979
I washed the little ones and cooked dinner.

Monday, April 30th 1979
I went to see Diane. I had an internal at family planning clinic. Three months tabs – Brevenor.

Tuesday, May 1st 1979
Dad going to Portsmouth

Sunday August 26th 1979
Dad has gone to Parkhurst Prison for one week.

Sunday, October 28th 1979
Visited Diane.

Wednesday, September 12th 1979
Dad told me mum has cancer (again) I just don't believe it, something is just not right.

Thursday, November 15th 1979
Dad has a nasty sore under his arm.

Monday, December 24th 1979
Went to see Diane. I miss her and wish she would come home.

Thursday, July 7th 2011
Today I am feeling like crap, in fact I've not felt right for over a week now. I don't want to be at work, I just want to be at home. I have spoken to Diane and I cried. I feel like a little girl lost and have a pain in my tummy and feel sick. Mentally I'm drained. I phoned the doctors today to arrange my smear test and I got upset. I asked if there was a mental health nurse at the surgery and the receptionist said I would need to see the doctor.

On a positive side at least I have noticed how I'm feeling. I know I need to take some time off from work. I spoke to Neil on Tuesday evening and cried. He said leave work, but I don't just want to leave. Every day is a struggle especially work days. So many people do not understand the affects that my childhood has had on me. I hope today I shall be ok. I think if anyone asks how I am I will cry.

Wednesday, July 13th 2011

I went for my smear test and bled as always. I spoke to the nurse about how I'd been feeling. I told her briefly about my book, my dad, my mum etc and I cried. She said it would be good to speak to the doctor, so I've made an appointment for the 25th of the month. I shall see how I go.

Monday, 26th December 2011

Today I feel lonely and sad. I feel that my husband and his mother do not want me around. I am not part of them. I am isolated and I do not join in with their conversation; when I do, I feel my contribution is not valid. I am not heard by his mother and he behaves differently around her. I might just as well not be here. Things are better when my children are here.

Thursday, January 5th 2012

Journal of Loss and Trauma

Shattered dreams, resiliency, and hope 'restoring' after loss.

Ted Bowman

I understand now, my dreams were shattered and lost. Deep within me a little voice said there is hope ... dream on.

CHAPTER THREE

Trying to Understand

EXPECTATIONS

When expectations about the course
of life are not met, people
experience inner chaos and disruption.
Such disruptions represent a loss of the future.
Restoring order to life necessitates reworking
understandings of the self and the world,
redefining the disruption and life itself.

Gay Becker

When I was very young, unbeknown to me, I was using natural coping mechanisms to block out the abuse I was suffering. This I now understand was a survival skill, a coping mechanism and, of course, it is now all starting to make sense. As a young child I couldn't afford to remember what was happening to me, so I blocked it out of my memory so that I could live through it. I was scared so I closed my eyes tightly shut.

Then years later in 1980, my repressed memories were triggered and re-emerged causing me considerable pain and anguish. For me, the commitment to an intimate relationship, the births of my children and the deaths of both my parents, have all been major triggers. Today, I have triggers on a daily basis that both consciously and unconsciously take me back to my childhood and early adult life. Most of these I now recognise and I have coping mechanisms in place to deal with them. Alternatively, I just ride them out, allowing the emotion and feelings to come and go. Sometimes these triggers are so powerful I behave in a way that is completely out of character. To onlookers this probably looks as though I've gone a little insane. I make no apologies for this strange and unusual behaviour as it is part of the person I have become. Recently a colleague at work said to me, 'Don't ever change the way you are'. If Kim knew half of what goes on in my head she would probably recommend I see a doctor, I'm sure.

It was only recently that I became aware of the connections between abuse and the current difficulties I face in my daily life. The effects of the childhood abuse have quite simply affected every single thing I do. I was relieved to find out that many of the problems and feelings I experience are just a natural result of an abusive childhood. Even to this very day I still have episodes of total despair. The damage to me was because of one person's selfish acts and I paid the price with the loss of an innocent childhood, which then carried on into my adult life.

Learning Curve – Time to Leave the Comfort Zone

As a child I had to protect myself from the emotional and physical horrors of abuse. In order to survive it, the child within me remained locked inside. I was unable to express my feelings and thoughts at that time and therefore these memories were not allowed to escape (locked deep inside my subconscious mind – a safe place), or so I thought. Years later these repressed memories were triggered by certain events and my adult mind could not cope or understand what was happening to me.

Counselling taught me about my recurring flashbacks, which are sometimes called Post Traumatic Stress Disorder (PTSD). Researching psychological trauma and the affects of repeated abuse has helped me to unravel and understand my own post traumatic stress. As a young child I was always on high alert, which I would have had no knowledge of or indeed understood at the time. This, I believe, caused physical and chemical changes within my brain which in turn altered my response to stress and certain situations. Although it was very upsetting to learn this, it did give me some of the answers as to why I behaved, felt and acted in certain situations. Situations where I feel threatened or under threat cause me to react impulsively; I am particularly sensitive if people come up behind me or stand too close.

One example is when I was fifteen years old I had a Saturday job working with my aunt in a bakery. The delivery driver had a habit of creeping up behind me and he found my over reaction to his advances rather funny. On one occasion I was making sandwiches and held a very large, sharp knife in my hand. The delivery man crept up on me and tried to grab both my hands. I moved away from him rather rapidly still holding the knife, which he grabbed accidentally instead my hands. As I moved, the knife sliced through the flesh on his palm resulting in a deep gash. The expression on his face was one of total shock. The next time he came into the shop he showed me the stitched scar and reminded me of exactly what I had done. 'Stupid sod' I thought, and from then on he gave me a wide berth. Although it was a complete accident, it worked, he never bothered me again.

The constant flashbacks I experienced were recollections from my past and although they had been frequent and scary before my counselling started, they became far more intense during the time of my counselling. I experienced sounds, smells, pictures and feelings, which made me feel panicky, trapped and powerless without understanding why. These experiences also happened during my dreams – my life was out of control.

I remember once Neil had gone through some of my belongings that I'd tucked away under my bed. I completely over-reacted and screamed at him totally out of control. It was an innocent action on his part but one that caused the inner me to go crazy.

I thought I was going insane and was afraid of telling anyone about what was happening to me. I started to avoid certain areas or situations that I believed would trigger my anger. Sometimes flashbacks would occur during any form of sexual contact, or just the way a person looked or behaved towards me would trigger memories of the individual who had abused me. Alternatively, it can be something quite ordinary that happens on a daily basis, stirring up similar trapped feelings.

This is the true story of my ongoing journey and the paths I have chosen to attempt to heal a broken soul. Writing this book about my life has been the most challenging, difficult and rewarding thing I have ever undertaken and I hope it can be an inspiration to others who have had been subjected to similar experiences.

Here are details of a very vivid flashback that I experienced in August 2008.

August 2008: If I Never See Your Face Again

I had decided to go and stay at my sister Diane's house. We had sat up talking for quite a long time until we felt it was time for bed. Diane showed me the room where I would be sleeping. I remember thinking it was very pink with dolls and teddies on the bed. It looked and felt like a proper girly bedroom which was something I had never had as a little girl. We had laughed in her bedroom as she showed me her new tilting bed. We acted silly like young girls and talked a little about our past, but I was happy and relaxed by the time I climbed into my bed.

I remember that I had no trouble getting off to sleep, but I woke at about 2.30 a.m. sweating and my heart was racing. As I rolled over I was aware that someone else was also in the bed and I froze. I lay very still, breathing deeply and trying to calm myself, listening for familiar sounds. I cannot describe the utter shock at seeing my father's face lying on the pillow next to mine as I turned over. I could smell his breath and actually feel it on my face. I nearly choked trying to hold back the screams that desperately wanted to erupt from my mouth. I was frozen in time, a time from long ago, a time that only I knew. I sobbed uncontrollably, trying to make sense of the whole situation. I felt sick, frightened and very alone. The affect of this flashback lasted for weeks.

I wonder will it ever go away. How can he still be here after all this time (fucking bastard)?

CHAPTER FOUR

A Little Bit of History

Building my Family Picture

My father was born in Gosport in Hampshire, the middle child having an older sister and a younger brother. His father was a skilled worker in the dockyard. My father claimed he was forced to do an apprenticeship as a plumber in a shipbuilding firm, but left there to join the army. After completing his five-year service he went into factory work. When I was born in 1959 he was working as a motor mechanic at Vauxhall Motors in Luton, earning somewhere between £16 and £20 per week. He worked a shift pattern which meant he was usually in the house during the day. When he came home from doing a nightshift during term-time, my mother would take my elder sister and brother to school and leave him in charge of me. The front door closes… the nightmare begins! I am a toddler, a child with my eyes tightly shut…

My mother was born and raised in Enfield in Middlesex. Her father worked for the railway. She was the baby of the family with five sisters and two brothers, all of whom adored her. Some of her family have described her as being a very gentle, loving and quiet person. She attended a secondary modern school and left at fifteen to work in a shoe shop. Her hobbies were machine sewing, swimming and walking. Before she married she worked at the Bellings factory and Yeoman's ticket factory in Enfield. The marriage to my father followed a two-year pen friendship while my father was serving in the army.

My parents married on the March 24th 1956 at St George's Church in Enfield.

I was born in the family home in the county of Hertfordshire on Wednesday, February 18th 1959. At the time of writing this I did not know how much I weighed or even what time I was born. There are no records of my birth in my mother's General Practitioner notes. Fortunately, I do have a birth certificate. I have memories of being washed in the bathroom sink; rough hands and splashes of tepid water covering my new, innocent body. I am the third eldest child of fourteen. I have eight sisters and five brothers and included in these are three sets of non-identical twins. We all have the same parents and my siblings are all alive to date and living in the UK.

* * * * *

Gaining access to my late mother's general practitioner notes in 2011 has been paramount to piecing the jigsaw together and learning about my early childhood. Discovering details about my siblings' births and the contributions they played in the family home over the years has filled me with deep emotions. I also took it upon myself to seek out and visit many elder relatives; each of whom gave me little snippets of valuable information.

I did a brief search in 2011 for my father's records and was informed that they had been destroyed. The records I have now hold key information about my mother's past, the deterioration of her health and the early years of my life. Generations come and go and once the information is lost or destroyed, it is gone forever. I believe the information I hold is priceless and I feel privileged, blessed and relieved that I hold it for safe-keeping in my possession for future generations. Included in these records are many other details and conversations that my mother had with her GP, but I have chosen not to include these.

I have had times when I have been on the brink of suicide because I thought I was going insane. For a short time I was prescribed antidepressants which did little to relieve the symptoms. On one occasion in 1990 I was out shopping in Peterborough with my husband and children. I left them browsing the shops and walked up the stairs of the multi-storey car park. I stood at the top preparing to jump off in an effort to try and stop the confusion that was permanently going around in my head. A lady approached me and asked me if I was ok? I simply replied 'No'. I can vaguely remember hearing cars, children's voices and doors slamming and then a voice came into my head and said, 'What are you doing, this is crazy?' I just stood there and cried – yes it was bloody crazy and I felt crazy, but I didn't for one minute understand what was happening to me. I was lost, alone and felt totally abandoned despite the fact that I had a loving family to whom I could have turned.

I had two separate occasions of general counselling before the specialist counselling in Cambridge. The general counselling gave me a chance to explore my feelings and inner grief. One of the counsellors actually suggested I leave my husband because she told me that I had 'married my mother'. After this suggestion, I explored the possibility that my husband was in fact quite like my mother, I was grasping at straws. He was furious when I told him and indicated that the counsellor obviously had it in for him and that she blatantly didn't like men.

* * * * *

In 2007 one of the first things I discussed with Helen from Choices was that I desperately wanted to empty my head. I needed to understand why I behaved in a certain way and why I was so unhappy. I felt ashamed, isolated and a complete failure. I truly believed that one day I would be admitted to hospital and be diagnosed with a mental disorder, just like my mother. At that time I simply didn't understand that the feelings and thoughts that I experienced every day of my life, were a normal response to abnormal events that had taken place throughout my childhood and early adult life. I would often feel totally detached and disassociated from the real world. Many times I would think to myself that I was meant to be alone and I didn't deserve to be loved. There are days now when I still feel the same – it is a long and slow healing process.

Happiness/Depression

There is no difference between happiness and depression. They both have the same process, it is just the content that is not the same. Both will come and go. The major difference between them is what we do with them.

We are always seeking happiness. When we see it coming we say: 'Ah, come here, I see you. Stay with me always'. Happiness laughs and says, 'Oh, she's/he's seen me, I can leave now'. And it does.

With depression, we see it coming, and we say: 'Go away, I don't want you. Not me'. And depression sighs and says, 'Here we go again, I'm going to have to get bigger and bigger for her/him to hear me and learn what I have to teach'. So it taps us on the shoulder and says, 'Over here, over here!' until it gets our attention. Then it leaves.

Both happiness and depression have something to teach us. Both will come and go. Both will return. It is our response and openness to learn from both that makes the difference.

My happiness is a gift.
My depression is a gift.
Both are like butterflies in my life
I must learn to accept them both equally

Ref: Anna Pavlova, from the book *Meditations For Women Who Do Too Much*, by Anne Wilson Shaef, 1990

CHAPTER FIVE

On Reflection

Not everything that is faced can be changed,
but nothing can be changed until it is faced.

James Baldwin

I was sitting in my bedroom and looking out of the window at the sky with nothing particular going round in my head except how lovely it was to think of nothing. I didn't want to be there in that house with my husband whom at the time I believed I hated. I wasn't happy but I didn't know why. I had often felt lonely even when I was surrounded by family and people who cared about me. For some strange reason I still felt as though I didn't belong. I found my mind wandering to a very peaceful place, somewhere far away. I thought of my mother and that she must have gone to this very place and decided to stay there in complete silence. At last I was at total peace. I wasn't even aware at the time that my husband had entered the room and had been observing me for quite some time.

My husband was so worried about me he telephoned the doctor. They didn't like the sound of my new vacant state and asked my husband to take me to the hospital straight away. I was aware of my husband's voice but it sounded as though he was miles away, when in fact he was sitting next to me on the bed. He held my hand and said we needed to go to the hospital as the psychiatrist would like to see me. In my head I thought, 'Oh well, they will understand what I'm going through and make me better'. I didn't know what else to do as I was in a complete state of limbo. I was aware of my children downstairs, I could hear them somewhere in my thoughts, but was not prepared to leave the sanctuary that I had found within my head. Then something snapped and I started to question myself and thought, 'I'm not bloody going to hospital. If the doctors want me they need to come and get me, because if I go in the car under my own steam they will think I'm ok.'

This for me was a turning point; I felt desperately alone and confused but I knew I needed help. I had previously been violent towards my husband and had even injured him when I lashed out. I knew this could not continue. I was suffering from Post Traumatic Stress Disorder (PTSD) and it was my father I was actually aiming my violent actions at but did not know it at the time. Sadly my husband took the full force of my anger. I felt totally mad and not at all in control of my actions. After each event I couldn't believe I had acted in such a violent way and was upset and distraught for a long time afterwards. My husband always remained calm; I've since learnt that he sometimes feared for his own life. This was no life for either of us and I was certainly no role model for my children.

During one of my violent episodes I had hit my husband with a bedside lamp while he was lying in bed. We had argued the previous evening and he had gone to bed ignoring me which made me furious. I got up at the usual time about seven a.m. while he had stayed in bed, still ignoring me. We were supposed to be going to stay at my sisters but he had said he didn't feel like going. Because of the ongoing trauma, he had also been put on prescription medicine to help him cope. I could feel the anger welling up inside me; I couldn't think straight and I hated him. I went up to our bedroom and he was lying under the covers with no intention of getting out of bed. I was thinking if he was dead I would be free, I wouldn't need to look at his ugly face again. I started shouting at him to get up. I wasn't seeing Neil's face at all I was looking at my father in bed (a flashback) but at the same time it was my husband – somehow I had no way of differentiating between the two. I picked the lamp up and Neil, seeing what was about to happen, held his arm up to protect his face. I was acting like a mad person, I totally lost control. Then I made my way into our en suite bathroom and completely smashed the place up. I threw all the toiletries in every direction, screaming and shouting that I didn't want to be here anymore.

My eldest son came into the bathroom and calmly asked what I was doing. I said, 'I don't know,' and started to cry uncontrollably.

On another occasion I actually sat in the kitchen holding a knife in my hand with a voice in my head telling me *I must kill my husband.* I am so thankful my husband has loved me enough and helped me to work through some of these most disturbing and terrifying times. Living with a person who has suffered trauma of any kind affects the people closest to them and it is too easy to forget that they also need to be heard. Our marriage has been a constant roller coaster of ups and downs.

My counsellor, Helen recommended *The Courage to Heal Workbook* and *Allies in Healing* by Laura Davis. Both books have been invaluable, not just for my own understanding of what was happening but also for my husband, the partner of an abuse survivor.

CHAPTER SIX

Progression

During my whole healing process I decided to take a course in (Neuro-Linguistic Programming) NLP. At school we are taught things like geography, history and biology but there is nowhere in the curriculum to teach us how to feel good about ourselves or how to handle relationships. This is where NLP comes in. It teaches you the skills of how to run your own life successfully and also the art of communication, something that was desperately lacking in my own life. During the course I was able to take part in some Time Line therapy in an effort to clear any repressed emotions. This helped me to recognise that my past was actually in front of me and that I needed to work through this to enable me to begin to move forward.

NLP and Typology – What makes me tick!

Now who'd of thought I wouldn't already know about ME! After all I've been on this planet for over forty years. I asked myself in 2007 who am I? What a question to asked oneself – but that's exactly what I did in NLP.

I shall explain very briefly my understanding of NLP. *Neuro* refers to our nervous system – the five senses of taste, touch, sight, hearing and smell. *Linguistic* is the language that we use, whether it is silent language as demonstrated in body language or phrases and words that we all use on a daily basis. Even when we are totally silent but perhaps have our arms and legs crossed, we are still communicating. *Programming*, we are basically a computer system (well not just, but you know what I mean). We all have our own map of the world inside our heads and our feelings, thoughts and actions are mostly habitual programs. These of course can be changed at any time. I believe that from a very young age we are bombarded with information, good or bad, which we then digest just like a computer. We are influenced by the people around us from the moment we are born; our parents, relatives, close friends, teachers and so on. This information we receive forms our values and belief system which we then unconsciously carry with us. Our beliefs start to change when, as young adults or even younger, we start to challenge and question them. For some people they never recognise that they have a belief system and they carry their outdated values and beliefs throughout there lives and stay firmly stuck in the past. As an example, a person may have been told that at six years old that they were no good at running. At sixteen, however, they win a cross country race but inside still believe they are rubbish. This is referred to as an outdated belief. Think about some of the things you believe about yourself and ask yourself are they outdated?

For me, learning about NLP opened a new chapter in my life. I completed the Practitioner course and now have a far greater understanding of what makes me and others tick. It has been a fabulous tool for using in my coaching practice and the results are always rewarding.

Discussing time was another eye opener. We all have very individual timelines (our language patterns give clues as to how we organise time internally). Some people say ‘stepping into the future’, ‘leaving old baggage behind’, ‘staying in the now’ or ‘this moment in time’, these are all familiar phrases.

What this tells us is that time is spatially around us and in NLP we call this timeline.

I did the following timeline exercise with a partner. We stood or sat with our eyes closed and were told to ask each other a series of questions. For example, I was asked to point to next week, last year's holiday, my future and my past. For me my past was just in front of my face and I held my hands to cover my eyes. This indicated that my past was holding me back from moving on and I had some issues that I needed to deal with. Perfectly true of course.

Another fascination of mine is personalities. Two amazing books that I read were *Beside Ourselves* (our everyday personality in everyday life by Naomi L. Quenk) and *Personality Type* (Typology by Lenore Thompson). I wanted to learn more about my own personality and completed a Myers-Briggs Type Indicator. This involves answering a series of questions which then gives you a description of your type. I completed the questionnaire and was surprised that mine was so accurate. There are sixteen personality types. We are all basically like a sandwich (sorry, trying to describe it as easily as possible). Imagine four slices of bread, each slice is a part of our personality.

1. The first slice is our primary attitude. Extraversion or Introversion.
2. The second slice is our approach to life. Sensation and Intuition.
3. The third slice is our Thinking and Feeling.
4. The fourth slice is our Perceiving or Judging.

So, we all have different extroverted and inferior parts to our personalities etc and all the slices can be muddled up depending on your own unique type which you will only discover if you should choose to take the test. For me I learnt that my third slice is a part of my personality that becomes very withdrawn at certain times and I like to be just left alone. For anyone witnessing me at that moment in time would probably think I was depressed, in actual fact I'm just having an inferior introverted time. I love it, just another little piece of me.

After all the progression and having learned so much about my inner self, I am now going to regress in the story and take you back to the time of my birth.

150 Knightsfield
The house where I was born

Where I was born

I was born in a three bedroom, semi-detached council house in Welwyn Garden City. The front door was painted bright yellow with the numbers 150 painted in black. Looking from the front of the house, on the left, stood a storeroom where father kept his bike, garden tools and a few other odds and sods. As you entered the front door you stepped into a small hall with stairs leading up from the right-hand side to three bedrooms – two at the front and one at the back overlooking the garden. Upstairs was also a bathroom and separate toilet. Downstairs there was a living/dining room and the kitchen which faced the sloping garden.

The house had a long, sloping front garden with steps and grasses on either side. I remember my father saying that he and a friend had stolen the paving slabs for the path from a new housing estate that was being built down the road. They had gone out one evening when it was dark and just helped themselves. At the side of the house in a small flowerbed my mother grew flag lilies and wallflowers and if I see them today they always remind me of her.

My brother and I would often swing on the neighbour's wire fence, back and forth, back and forth, that was until my brother cut his mouth on the wire. That soon stopped that bit of fun. Albert the next door neighbour erected a fence to keep us children out.

Mother would never eat with us because my father insisted that she had her meal on her own first and then we would be allowed to have ours; a fact that an aunt clarified only recently. A neighbour's garden backed onto the bottom of ours where they grew gooseberries and blackcurrants which were very

Denise at approximately three years

tempting to a small child. I remember putting my fingers through the fence and helping myself to the delicious fruit.

The naughtiest thing I ever remember doing at that house was peeing in a rusty old paint tin which had been left around the side of the house for disposal. My older brother and sister promised they wouldn't tell on me if I did it, but needless to say, children being children, they did and I had a darned good hiding from my father. I remember to this day he called me 'a dirty girl'.

If I looked across the road from our front garden I could see Sherrards Wood. This was, and still is today, a beautiful area of woodland with never-ending paths to explore, a great place for children to have adventures.

On a school day my older brother and I would walk past an old, gnarled oak tree. Part of the tree had grown in such a way that it looked like a door and as children we would pretend someone actually lived in the tree. There was a play park not far from our house, also in Sherrards Wood, and, when allowed, we would spend time there unsupervised. I had two accidents falling from the roundabout, crashing to the muddy, stony ground. My left arm still bears the scars of both falls.

School days

I loved to go to school when I was five years old and my first day at Harwood Hill School was on Monday 20th April 1964. I had a brand new satchel and I remember it was a gorgeous conker brown colour. It was my pride and joy and I would spend a lot of time just undoing the buckles and doing them up again. Most days I walked with my older brother to and from school, up a long hill and crossing two roads before we arrived back home. Mother sometimes stood in the front garden waiting for our return. I stayed at this school for just over a year and my final day was on the 18th June 1965.

The second school I attended was Nutfield infants, followed by Rowans mixed junior school. I remember it took me a long time to learn to read the *Janet and John* books and telling the time was another difficult lesson. Actually I learnt to tell the time with ease, I just pretended I couldn't because I liked to spend time with the lady teacher. I think she knew but never said.

When I started infant school, again I would sometimes walk with my elder brother. I remember him winning a jar of sweets in a 'guess how many sweets are in the jar' competition. If I remember correctly I believe he guessed that there were one hundred and eighty-nine sweets in the jar. His face was an absolute picture as he ran up the hill carrying the jar. He was so proud. I was excited and proud too because he was my brother.

My elder sister Sharon went to a different school from my brother and I, although at the time I didn't know why. I only found out later that the school we attended had not been built when my sister came of school age. I remember on one occasion going with my father to collect her. My father picked me up and placed me on the wall outside the school. I remember the wall being very high – how lucky was I?

As a very young child when I heard the *Magic Roundabout* tune I knew it was nearly six o'clock and time for bed. During the week it was always the same, no bedtime story, just off to bed. Lying in bed I could sometimes hear the *Coronation Street* theme tune and also sounds of shouting. The shouting and muffled voices, however, were not coming from the black and white television set. I would hold my hands over my ears and close my eyes tightly shut. The house was dark but it was never silent. Clicking knees on the stairs, footsteps in my bedroom and hands under the covers…

I know a little girl
Who had a little curl
Right in the middle of her forehead
When she was good
She was very, very good
But when she was bad, she was horrid.

By Henry Wadsworth Longfellow 1807-1882

My father would often repeat this poem to me.

CHAPTER SEVEN

The Family is Growing

My older sister Sharon was born at Chase Farm Hospital, Enfield in February 1957. She weighed 6lb 8oz and was breastfed successfully by my mother. The following February my older brother was born in the Maternity Hospital in Pear Tree Lane, Welwyn Garden City. He weighed 8lb 5oz and was also breastfed. I arrived a year later and was the only child from our family to be actually born in the family home. I have yet to find details in my mother's records regarding my actual birth. A thorough search for records relating to visits from midwives or health visitors during the time of my birth was inconclusive. I have to say I was disappointed but not surprised.

I remember vividly when the first set of twins arrived. They came home in an ambulance. Two tiny cots were placed on the living room floor; a little boy inside one and a little girl in the other. The baby boy weighed 6lb 6oz and the little girl 7lb 2oz, they were both bottle fed. I was fifteen months old and the year was 1960; my abuse had already started. Now we were a family of seven and I remember having chicken pox at about this time. I have a memory of standing in a cot and crying, but no one came, no hugs, no comforting and no time for me.

In September 1961 the second set of twins were born. The boy was a breech birth and weighed 8lb 2oz. The girl was a forceps birth and weighed 7lb 2oz. These two beautiful, round, chubby-faced babies, as written in the report, would never come home from the hospital to our house. Instead they stayed in the hospital for a while, while mum continued to care for them for about ten days. She fed them, bathed them and bonded with them. However, after this short, but memorable time for her, they were fostered out on October 10th 1961; something that must have been a very hard decision for my mother to make.

Letter written by the Children's Officer on October 27th 1961

> Mrs Arm was expecting twins, she already had five children under the age of five and both her and her husband felt they could not cope with another set of twins. I saw them several times before and after the babies were born.
>
> The Child Care Officer writes that she had seen Mrs Arm several times after she had had the babies and she did not waiver in her decision to have them adopted. She had handled them herself and said she knew she was giving the adopters two lovely children. She was discharged from the hospital at ten days. I saw Mr and Mrs Arm before the babies were placed for adoption. We went over all the reasons for and against adoption and the Arms did not go back on their original decision. They could see that the twins would have a much better start in life than they could give them. Mrs Arm was advised not to have any more children and is getting advice about this as further pregnancies are likely to endanger her health.

I saw Mrs Arm a fortnight or so after the babies had been placed in the Watford area. She was certain she had done the right thing in having the babies placed for adoption as she was finding her own children quite a handful. Her other twins of 17 months were at a very exhausting stage and she found her time was completely taken up with them and the other children. She was pleased to hear that the twins were doing so well with their new carers and she said then that she thought she would be able to give her consent as would her husband.

I have recently enquired from the Health Visitor Mrs Oesawka about Mrs Arm and apparently now she is feeling the guilt of giving up the babies more strongly. I was going to arrange for the Arms to sign the consent forms, but it seems that it would better for them if this was delayed for a couple of weeks for them to sort their feelings out. I will advise when I think it is safe to approach Mrs Arm.

According to reports that I obtained recently, by November of that year my mother was feeling increasingly guilty for allowing her babies to go up for adoption. Because she was so distressed, it was decided by the childcare officer to delay the signing of the consent forms for a few weeks. This was allegedly to give my mother some time to sort her feelings out.

On January 17th 1962 a review report was sent to the Hertfordshire Children's Committee. The Child Care Officer visited my parents on January 26th 1962 to assess their attitude to the adoption. On that day my parents signed the final papers and, according to the officer, seemed relatively happy about doing this.

She wrote:

> I visited the Arms on the 24th of January to assess their attitude to the adoption. Unfortunately the Guardian Ad Litem from the probation department had visited the previous day so I was not able to prepare them for this. Despite this, however, the Arms had signed the final papers and seem relatively happy about this. They have made friends with Mr Arm's family recently with the exception of his sister who still feels the adoption was unwise. They have their hands full with the other five children especially as at the moment Mrs Arm is trying to potty train the twins.
>
> Mrs Arm herself was looking much better than on previous occasions. The Arms were quite definite that they would not have any more children, and I later discussed this with the health visitor who said she was arranging for Mrs Arm to attend the family planning centre. She hoped that this would prove successful as we both feel that now Mrs Arm could very easily become pregnant again due to the feelings of the loss of the twins.

My mother at this time was busy with five young children and also potty training the two older twins. This I can only imagine from my own experiences would have been a full time job. I was still only two years and eleven months old.

My father had rented a washing machine around this time which would have made things a little easier. Up until then my mother had done it all by hand often making her hands bleed after a day of washing, scrubbing and rinsing. I believe the washing machine was only rented for a very short time due to the state of their finances and mother had to return to washing by hand, a chore that many of her daughters would eventually take on. The first washing machine I remember was after I met my future husband. His mother was getting a new machine and she gave us her old twin tub and small spin dryer. This was a special gift from Neil's parents and very much appreciated.

As a child I used to clean the house, not that there was much to clean – brush the stairs, sweep the floors. When I was very little mum would sometimes sprinkle hundreds and thousands on the living room carpet. We would pick each tiny sugar strand up and eat it. This sometimes seemed to take forever but it gave us the greatest pleasure. I think mum did it to keep us quiet.

At this time both my parents had said they would definitely not have any more children and the health visitor was making arrangements for my mother to attend the family planning clinic. My mother was advised against having any more children, as any further pregnancies were likely to endanger her health.

Years later I would trace both the adopted twins…

Family Planning Association July 16th 1962

Dear Dr Lloyd,

Re: Mrs D Arm

I thought you would like to know that the pregnancy test on this patient was positive.
Twin pregnancy confirmed by x-ray.

Despite the advice my mother was once again confirmed to be pregnant by x-ray in the latter half of 1962. On the notes it said my mother refused routine admission for rest due to 'domestic reasons'. The following year on Wednesday, January 9th 1963 my mother gave birth to twin girls. The first twin weighed 5lb and was a breech delivery and the second weighed 6lb 8oz, she was a normal delivery. At this time I would have been three years and eleven months old. We were now an extended family of nine.

In early March 1963 according to records, my mother attended the family planning clinic for contraceptive advice. She decided she would prefer the contraceptive pill and started taking this on March 29th 1963.

In late October 1964 my mother was seen by her GP after suffering two severe attacks of tonsillitis in three weeks. In the second case she had developed quinsy (a condition similar to tonsillitis) on the left side of her throat. As a child she had had her tonsils removed but consular remnants remained. It was agreed by an ENT registrar that she should have the remnants removed and she was placed on the waiting list, but I do not know if she actually went on to have the operation.

Our house must have been hectic. Having had three children myself I can imagine what it must have been like for my mother. The first set of twins (Diane and Kevin) were fostered out for a five-month period when they were fifteen months old and then again later for a shorter spell – Mum's brother and wife looked after them in Hertford. Speaking to my uncle recently, I learned that my mother never visited them during this time and my father only went twice. According to my uncle the twins never went to my father willingly, they seemed to prefer my aunt and uncle. Not surprising really as they would have been very well fed and cared for.

This time apart would have given my mother a little respite. She was still doing all the washing by hand and I have fond memories of her delicious rabbit stew and toffee. I can see her now standing in the front garden as my brother and I came home from school. Mum would be waiting for us with a smile that held a thousand stories.

In December 1967 and January 1968 my mother was admitted to hospital in false labour. She was later discharged. On Wednesday, February 7th 1968 my mother gave birth to a 10lb 3oz girl. The delivery was normal.

My mother attended the ante-natal clinic on January 22nd 1969 and on this visit the doctor advised her that she should be sterilised following her last pregnancy. He stated in his notes that he felt she was rather 'dim' and thought it unlikely that she would agree to this operation.

On Tuesday, July 9th 1969 she was admitted to hospital in early labour. Labour was not established and she was discharged home on the 10th. On Friday, July 12th 1969 she gave birth to her eleventh child, a daughter, at 10.40 am. The birth was normal and the little girl weighed 8lb 13oz. Or should I say, not so little. Mum chose the name Sandra for the baby because her ex-neighbour at 150 had named their daughter Sandra and mum loved the name.

CHAPTER EIGHT

Good Times, Bad Times

Ticket to ride

I was about five or six years old when I travelled to Portsmouth with my father on the train. I'd been given a bag sweets and I felt very special, mainly because I'd been the one chosen to go and no one else. I loved the train and the different noises as it travelled over the tracks. I would look out the window and watch the ever-changing landscape flashing by and the darkness as the train passed through a tunnel. Travelling on trains today is always a trigger and transports me back to my childhood and time spent with my father.

I didn't much like my grandmother; she was short, petite and always seemed to be cross. I remember that when she had a cup of tea, she always had two rich tea biscuits. She held the biscuits in her hand in a way that you wouldn't even know she had them. I would ask her what she had in her hand, and she would turn her hand slowly showing me the biscuits. She always wore an apron, her hair was grey, cut into a short style with a bit of a curl and she wore glasses. I was frightened of her and did my very best to keep out of her way; in some ways she reminded me a little of my father.

Granddad, on the other hand, was different and I really liked him. He seemed kind and had a gentle nature. I have since learned, however, that he had quite a temper. Granddad wore glasses, was tall and well built. He wore grey trousers, a shirt and pullover and his hair was also grey, a whitish grey that used to be combed to one side. He had a lovely garden with lots of different plants growing in it and I was always happy to follow him outside; anything to get away from my grandmother. On this particular visit granddad said he had some things to show me outside and I followed him as usual. It was a bright, warm, sunny day. We looked at a few things in the garden and he walked into his shed and, being an innocent child, I just followed. Once inside he pushed the door shut and I immediately began to feel uncomfortable. I remained quiet and stood still, my arms pushed down hard against my sides. On the top of the shelves he had some magazines; he reached up and took one down. As he came towards me I saw that his trousers were open and he started pushing himself against me. He had an erection; I was so small and he started talking, saying, 'Come on'. I had no idea what he meant I just wanted to get out. I managed to reach for the door and made my escape back into the open air of the garden. Things would never be the same again between my grandfather and me. I didn't look back once I was inside the house. I felt totally isolated and couldn't make any sense of what had just happened. I couldn't tell my grandmother or father what had just taken place in the shed. Granddad came into the house a short while later and everything was just the same as if nothing had ever happened. This sad and shocking experience I kept to myself for over twenty years.

Growing Up at 56

Growing up at 56, that was the house number at Lumbards in Welwyn Garden City, Hertfordshire. My father painted an eye on the wall behind one of the pictures and as he left the house he would say, 'I'm always watching you and I always know what you're doing'. This is one of my earliest memories. As a small child the seed had been sown by my father, 'I am watching you always'. To this very day, I am filled with painful, deep emotions that are unconsciously triggered, if I catch a glimpse of someone watching me.

Innocence

He was an evil, sadistic man and yet he could charm just about anyone. His life was one big lie, and the more lies he told the more he needed to tell to get out of what he'd already said. He was a true Jekyll and Hyde character. I was petrified of him, I hated him and yet I still loved him. I wanted to be loved, nothing more, nothing less. I named my youngest son after my father because I thought this would make him proud of me, what a fool I was.

I don't ever recollect either of my parents ever telling me they loved me. As far as my father was concerned I was a waste of space. He would tell me, 'You're all mouth and trousers' time and time again until I started to believe it. He would tell me I was like a leaf in the wind and that he never knew what mood I would be in. He'd say he felt sorry for the poor sod who ended up marrying me. One of my sisters received a bereavement card from him when she married, that is how warped his mind was.

Dad gave mum Tic Tacs instead of her medication; the hospital suspected this but did nothing about it.

When I was about nine years old my mother came to the top of the stairs and was shouting, 'I've got no legs, no legs, help me'. I had no idea what was going on. I could hear her talking to herself so I ran upstairs and found her looking out of her bedroom window. She was saying, 'They are coming to get me look they are outside'. I looked out of the window and could see no one. I said to her, 'There's no one there'. She stared back at me crying with a vacant expression on her face. I don't remember who else was present in the house at the time. Looking back now I wonder if she was suffering with post-natal depression.

Sometimes she would buy men's shirts; but these were not for my father. The shirts would be folded neatly and laid out on her bed and when my father thanked her she replied, 'They are not for you'. They were in actual fact for a different male visitor. Before my mother met my father she had a crush on another young man who she used to babysit for. According to the information within her GP notes she had loved this man deeply and he apparently felt the same way about her. Her father, however, for unknown reasons had abruptly ended the relationship and her heart was broken. I don't think she got over her broken heart and had spoken to her doctor, confiding in him. This doctor was a man she knew and trusted and I know from my own memories she was very fond of him.

On occasion I would go with my mother to visit her parents who lived in Enfield. We always went by bus which we caught from the main station in Welwyn Garden City. On one particular return trip for some reason we got off the bus too early; mum was confused and we were lost. I remember feeling the most peculiar emotions and thinking how can she not know where we are. For a while I didn't know what to do and just stood in a state of limbo. I took control of the situation, but wasn't aware of it at the time (I must have been only eight or nine years old). I told my mother that we needed to find a telephone box and I remember looking for the bright red landmark. We walked around for a while and I made sure that I held my mother's hand tightly until we eventually came across a telephone box. Between the two of us we managed to dial our home number and explain that we were lost. I remember looking out of the telephone box for a street sign so that I could tell them exactly where we were. Many years later I learned that we were only a few stops away from the town centre. My mother was clearly unwell at this time and that was the very last time we visited her parents. I remember her parents fondly even though I hardly ever saw them.

The School Trip

In October 1969 I was ten years old and went with my mother on a school trip to Covent Garden in London. I had never been to London, so this was an adventure in itself. We were going to the opera to see La Bohème. We were only allowed to go because my teacher said he would take care of my mother – not me please note, my mother. I knew she wasn't very well, but didn't know exactly what was wrong with her. We travelled from the school on a coach to London and I sat next to my mum. We had ice cream and for the first time in a long while I felt happy and normal, just like the other children on the coach. My mum was thirty-three years old.

Some Concerns

In November 1969 mother had confided to her doctor that she believed one of her sons had been stealing at school. She told him that he had given a teacher some cigarettes and chocolate. Mother said he was a terror because he had broken the door and torn up the floor. At first I had smiled inwardly because she had been able to tell her doctor the story, but after some thought I had remembered the episode of her shouting that she had no legs – a figment of her imagination but nonetheless very real to her at the time.

Mother stopped taking her medication because she'd run out.

In a letter dated February 13th 1970 a senior social worker had written to my mother's GP. In the letter the social worker had voiced her concerns over my mother's condition. It would seem that she had visited her on that day and that it was the first time she had seen her that year. She had said my mother had lost some of her organisation. The washing had piled up because my mother said she had been unable to visit the launderette. She pointed out that with a family of eleven my mother really needed to be well organised. There were no sheets for the children's beds and she had no nappies for the baby and was using dirty pillowcases instead. The senior social worker had also written that my mother was easily distracted in a psychotic sort of way and seemed very preoccupied with what goes on around her and was rather bewildered by it.

I shudder, am upset and appalled as I read this. It is August 2011 and I have received my mother's GP notes and this is just one small piece of information from her notes which was signed by a Senior Social Worker. She left my mother with washing piled high, no sheets on our beds and dirty pillowcases for nappies. The social worker said she felt my mother's condition had deteriorated since the first time she saw her. I am saddened by this report but it is another tiny piece of the jigsaw, the puzzle of my early life starting to take shape and fit together.

The Wedding

I travelled by train with my mother and one of my brothers to attend a family wedding in Portsmouth. My uncle was getting married and my father was to be the best man. My elder sister and father had travelled ahead of us because my sister was having a fitting for her bridesmaid dress.

When we arrived at my grandparent's house apparently my grandmother was not happy that our shoes were rather worn. She took my brother and I into the town and bought me a new pair of white sandals and some new shoes for my brother. I was delighted and so proud to have a new pair of shoes.

I was staying at my auntie's house and sharing a bed with my father, something which filled me with dread. I also remember feeling cross that my sister had been chosen as a bridesmaid instead of me. She was so much prettier than me, with her dark hair and dark eyes and I thought she was clearly the favourite. I on the other hand, had crazy hair, was on the chubby side and altogether a bit of a wild child.

I was bought a pair of new shoes on another occasion during a visit to my grandparents in Portsmouth. I didn't get many new things as a child, especially new shoes, so these shoes were very, very special. The shoes were made of dark red and black suede with black and white stripy laces. The best thing of all was that they were MINE! As bedtime approached I was starting to think about other stuff, I hated the dark and I certainly didn't want to share a bed with my father. I remember making such a fuss because I wanted the door left open when I went to bed. Maybe unconsciously I thought I would be safe if the door was open. My auntie said if the door was left open the Siamese cats would come in and chew my new shoes. I remember crying, shouting and making such a commotion that in the end the door was left slightly ajar. It was a small comfort because I could see a faint light when I finally climbed into bed, totally exhausted. My father got into bed sometime later and although I had my back to him I could still smell him. He moved closer and I moved away … I drifted off to sleep with my eyes tightly shut.

On waking the next morning the first thing that went through my mind were my new shoes. I looked at them on the floor and to my horror, just as my auntie had predicted, the laces had been chewed; they didn't look like laces anymore. I was inconsolable. I cried, I screamed, I went on and on and on. All my auntie and father kept saying was, 'We told you they would be chewed if the door was left open.' Only now years later do I understand the cruelty and nastiness of both their actions. I was only a child. They could have so easily put the shoes in another room and closed the door. Because of the fuss I had caused, my father and auntie took me into town to buy replacement laces. We went from shop to shop looking for black and white stripy laces without any luck. I hated them both. In the end my auntie bought plain black laces which were far too long. (*Bitch*)

How to Survive

In order to survive I lived in my own little world, totally detached and disassociated from the real world. I would pretend that when I was dreaming in my sleep that that was the real world, and during the day the real world was just a dream. I learned from a very tender age to keep quiet and still, to watch and to not make a sound. I would watch people, studying their every move – the way they sat, what they said and how they moved. As I got older I was referred to by my father's family as the ONE that told lies and couldn't be trusted. I hated all of them; I was definitely the black sheep of the family, the odd one out. In a strange sort of way I have always known I was different.

Today I am still fascinated by people and their behaviour and I love to people watch. Running my own life coaching business is immensely rewarding because I get to see the changes in people and the difference I can make to someone's life. It is very rewarding especially as I have moved so far forward with regard to my own life.

Move to Haldens 1965

Sometime in 1965 we moved to a new four-bedroomed house in Haldens, Welwyn Garden City. I remember our black Silver Cross double pram and the journey to and fro with the few possessions we owned, taking them from the old house to the new. The twins were asleep in the pram, mum pushing and us children trying to keep up. The journey seemed to take forever. We walked over the bridge which the railway ran beneath. I couldn't see the trains as I was too small, I just heard and felt them as they rumbled beneath my feet. We walked past rows of houses, a new shopping centre and finally arrived at our new house.

The house, as I remember, was enormous with an alleyway dividing next door from ours. We had a garden with an outhouse which housed a coal bunker and at the bottom of the garden was a waste patch of land.

Inside the house there were two reception rooms, a kitchen, a hallway and toilet. Upstairs were four bedrooms and a bathroom. I ran through all the rooms; the house seemed alive with echoes of voices and sounds bouncing off the newly-plastered walls. I don't know if I got to choose my bedroom, I very much doubt it.

An early memory of mine was waking during the night when the electricity meter had run out of coins. I called out several times saying the tanner had run out, but was simply told by my father to 'shut up'. I was frightened of the dark in those days even though the house was full of noise. I shared a bed with different sisters over the years, using the top and tail system to give us more room. There were never any bedcovers to keep us warm, just my black duffle coat. It wasn't until I was a teenager that I had my own bed and when I married I had my very first pillow. On one occasion I remember asking a sister to move over as I felt cramped. She replied, 'I'm already at the wall'. I kicked my sister Mandy that night and she had the most awful bruise on her calf in the morning.

The Good, the Bad and the Ugly

I became a mother to my younger siblings at the tender age of nine or ten. I didn't want to be a mother with all the responsibilities, it just happened. I grew up thinking this was quite normal. When I was attending counselling in my forties I remember discussing with my counsellor an issue I was having with a sibling. My counsellor asked me how old the sibling was, when I gave her the age she replied, 'Oh, so they are over twenty-one?'

'Yes', I replied.

Sitting for a while in silence it then dawned on me that this sibling was in fact an adult and it wasn't my responsibility to be mothering or trying to take responsibility for them. It has taken me nearly a lifetime to recognise this. It had been drummed into me from such an early age by my father, it just felt normal to always look out for them and help as best I could with whatever difficulties they may be having. I suddenly realised that I had always put myself second. It's not easy just stopping this behaviour but at least I now recognised it.

After the third set of twins was born in January 1963, I

believe my mother was on the contraceptive pill for five years. I can't imagine my father would have taken any precautions to stop her from getting pregnant. In some of the documents that I have, there is some suggestion that he had agreed to a sterilisation, but needless to say he never did go ahead with the procedure. Some of my mother's family have confirmed this. Once while going through my mother's drawers I found a contraceptive cap, although I wasn't sure at the time what it was as I was only eight years old. Mother had no other babies until February 1968 when a little girl arrived. The baby girl was beautiful. I was nine years old. Over the next six years another four babies were born.

'I need a vestie.' This was a funny thing one of my younger brothers would say when he was feeling cold. He hadn't quite mastered how to say the word 'vest'.

Mud Hills 1967/68

Sometimes I would play behind our house on the waste patch of land. If dad wasn't in I'd climb over our fence, if he was in and I was allowed to go out, I'd walk to the disused road that joined the waste land. Huge mounds of mud covered the central area and it was named the mud hills. Around the outside of the mud hills was a grassy no-man's land. A friend of my father had given my elder sister and I an old secondhand adult bike. It was dark maroon in colour and looked enormous to a nine-year-old child. However, I was determined to ride it and after several unsuccessful attempts I managed to pedal it and rode over the mud hills. This was a whole new adventure for me and I rode it whenever I got the chance. I actually rode it until the damn thing fell to pieces. I don't think my sister Sharon rode it as much as I did.

The lady who gave us the bike was a colleague of my father and I remember her coming to the house to look at some of his paintings. When he was in a good mood he would paint pictures in oils. The paintings were usually of landscapes and sometimes boats out at sea. This lady came into our house and didn't even acknowledge my existence. I remember thinking what a large nose she had. Her hair was dark, short and she wasn't particularly attractive. I watched her for a while pretending to be interested in his art work and joking with my father. I wasn't fooled by them for one moment, I knew exactly what was going on between them. The silent gestures said it all and I remember hating my father even more on that day. My mother conveniently was in hospital at the time.

When the mud hills were flattened in the early 1970s to make way for a new housing development, wild grasses and flowers began to grow where the ground was originally barren. I loved that place. I'd make a pretend house out of stones, placing each stone in a line to form the outside of each room. I always had a four bedroomed detached house with two bathrooms. In the kitchen I would make meals for my family and, when I was joined by my other siblings, they would be served the imaginary food in the stone dining room. I would lay on my back in the sunshine in my make-believe house and garden. I loved to listen to the skylarks as they flew high above me in the clear blue skies. This was my world, a place where I could feel safe and free.

However, the time eventually came for the new houses to be built. Fences were erected and it became a no-go area for children; my beautiful world, my safe haven, had been destroyed. I worried where the skylarks would go. As if by magic the new houses were built and occupied in the blink of an eye. They were detached with en-suite bathrooms and tiny little postage stamp gardens. People living in little boxes and all the houses looking the same.

I used to dream that one day I would live in a cottage with a beautiful garden full of birds and wildlife. I would have four children and a gentle, kind man would sleep next to me. There would always be hot water, soft towels, food in the fridge, a bed with pillows and white linen. Of course I would live happily ever after in my make-believe world.

On occasions my elder brother would let me tag along when he went bird nesting. I loved climbing the trees; I suppose I was a bit of a tomboy. If we found any eggs we would pierce them with a needle and blow the yoke out. Sometimes you'd get a rotten one and it would stink. They were then proudly placed between cotton wool in a drawer in the outhouse. I would check the eggs every day. They were delicate, fragile and beautiful and I knew which bird species each and every egg came from.

Hold fast to dreams
For if dreams die
Life is a broken-winged bird
That cannot fly.
Hold fast to dreams
For when dreams go
Life is a barren field
Frozen with snow.

Langston Hughes

Scraps From the Chip Shop and Stolen Biscuits

Oh how I loved school dinners, free school meals.

In the juniors a boy had come to school with chocolate buttons with hundreds and thousands on. He was showing his friends in the playground before school started and I remember thinking how desperately I wanted the sweets. I'd had no breakfast and was really hungry. During the morning lesson I asked to go to the toilet. The toilets were directly next to the cloak room. I knew which coat belonged to the boy and I put my hand in the pocket and took the sweets out. I put them into my pocket and went back into class. When it was morning break the boy started to cry and said that someone had stolen his sweets. The plan was that I would eat them before anyone noticed, unfortunately there wasn't time. We were all made to line up and everyone was asked by the teacher if they had taken them. When the teacher asked me I said, 'Yes, I took them'. If I'd been taught anything by my father it was to always speak the truth.

I was escorted unceremoniously to the headmaster's office. He asked me why I'd taken the sweets and I told him that I was hungry. He enquired what had I had for breakfast and I replied, 'Nothing'. The headmaster took me to the tuck shop and gave me permission to select a snack. I was shocked and didn't know what to choose, eventually deciding on a packet of potato tube things. I apologised to the boy and gave him his sweets back. I could not have predicted the outcome and I remember being so relieved that my father would not have to find out. I didn't care what the other children thought, I was happy to have something to eat. Looking back, maybe the teacher knew that my life wasn't as much fun as some of the other children in my year.

There was never enough to eat at home when I was growing up. The local fish and chip shop was a good place to go because I could always get the scrapes from the bottom of the frying pan. Even to this day I love the crunchy small chips. The local supermarket was also a good place to get a free packet of biscuits. When the shop was closed I would lay on my belly on the cold concrete with a long stick and poke it through the letter box. With precision I would knock a packet of biscuits from the lower shelf and ease them to the letter box, always a treat.

Some days the larder was completely empty and that is why I loved the free school meals. I would never waste anything and if there were second helpings I'd always be there with my plate. The school meals at junior school were always served from hot stainless steel tins. Children would take turns at serving the food out. I particularly liked the carrots as they tasted amazingly sweet. I never felt ashamed or embarrassed at receiving the free school meals, they were a godsend and for me the highlight of the day. Sometimes on the way home from junior school I'd stop and steal a rose or two for my mum from someone's garden, but not before I checked to see if anyone was watching. She always smiled when I gave them to her, so the small risk was always worthwhile to just see her face light up.

During the school holidays at home, if we were lucky, sometimes there was fat dripping to spare, delicious spread on white bread, or occasionally white bread with sugar on. If there was any milk spare we would have that on the white bread too. Before mother was ill I remember her cooking rabbit stew and making toffee, it was such a treat. We would never be allowed to leave the table until our plates were clean but we were always so hungry we would lick our plates until not a single morsel of food remained.

On one occasion one of my sisters had to sit at the table for hours until she had finished her meal. I remember her not liking the food on her plate, she just kept crying, but dad made her sit there until her plate was empty. I lost count of how many clips round the ear she received on that day.

Dad had rules; we were never allowed to buy margarine. My father always had butter which was solely his property. I remember buying margarine once, believing that I was saving him money, but dad just opened the dining room window and threw it out. He was swearing and shouting, saying it was 'fucking rubbish'. He said he was going to make me eat the whole packet to teach me a lesson. I feel sick now just thinking about it. Needless to say I never bought margarine again. He was such a bastard; he always had the best sausages, pies and Cracker Barrel cheese – I always went without.

On one occasion Diane had been sent to buy a packet of Ariel washing powder and by mistake she'd bought a bar of Aero chocolate instead. Not only did she get a hiding for not listening, she was beaten soundly for eating the chocolate. To this day I'm not bothered by food. When I was earning money, Diane sometimes would run an errand for me to buy Ski yogurts, Camp coffee and fruit. I don't ever remember eating much at home. Most weeks at some point we would have mashed potato with raw egg and another dish was cheese pie. Not a lot of cheese, if the truth be known, just egg.

The ice cream van would pass by in the summer blaring out tunes enticing children to taste its wares. Sometimes mum would have an oyster ice cream and as a very special treat (I can only remember this happening once), we'd buy a block of ice cream and it would be divided between all twelve of us. The best part was licking the cardboard, every last drop, yummy.

Christmas and the Dolly Hello/Goodbye 1966

At Christmastime in our house we always had a Christmas meal. One year the oven door was broken and had been for some time, so we had to wedge a chair under the handle and this did a reasonable job of keeping the door closed. We have had Christmas lunches where the turkey was undercooked and we all ended up with food poisoning. On another occasion the turkey was so large we had to cut the legs off to get it into the oven. As we got older, the meal would be divided into two sittings.

When mum was well in the very early years she would make Christmas cake and pudding and as children we were allowed to take turns to stir the mixture and then make a wish. She added a sixpence to the pudding mixture and if you were lucky enough to find it that was magic, but I am afraid I never found the sixpence.

On Christmas morning we would not be allowed to go downstairs until everyone had used the bathroom and mum was dressed. We would queue at the top of the stairs, the eldest going down first. The anticipation of what I might get was overwhelming. When dad said we could go down the stairs we would follow the person in front. Slowly and carefully walking down and trying not to make too much noise. Many times we would be sent back up the stairs because we were making too much noise. Then we would have to start the process all over again. The eldest child going first and so on. When we finally arrived at the living room door we would go in one at a time to receive our gifts. In my minds eye the room is dull and grey and strangely coloured wrapped gifts await us. Usually a small pile of presents, each pile laid out neatly next to the other. I would wait to be told by my father which pile was mine, hoping and praying it was the largest. One Christmas when I was about six years old I was given a dolly from Father Christmas. She was wrapped in a box with a cellophane window. I can see her now, she was small with brown hair tied into bunches and she had screwed up fists. Her face had tiny freckles on both cheeks and dad told me the dolly was cross just like me. My elder sister Sharon and Diane were also was given a dolly, but they were different to mine.

Christmas day passed and I looked for my dolly but couldn't find her anywhere. I asked my parents if they had seen her and they both replied 'no'. I couldn't understand what had happened to her. I wondered if she had been put in the loft, it was the only place left that I could think of. I couldn't get into the loft and begged my dad to go and look for her. I was quite distraught. My sisters also lost their dolls and I can only assume now that the dolls were taken back to the shop. I have often thought about my special dolly and what had happened to her. The search for that dolly continues to this day, I search e-bay, charity shops and car boot stalls in the hope that one day she may turn up.

Christmas for me was an unhappy time. It seemed people everywhere were celebrating a family occasion, but I always felt something wasn't quite right. It was false because the rest of the year was horrid.

A Little Boy's Finger

Why was it always me that had to look after the little ones? I didn't want to look after my younger siblings every day during the school holidays, I wanted to be out having fun. This particular day was no different. I now know that sometimes they didn't like it either, as I wasn't always very nice to them. I would hit them or chase them with the broom and I once pushed my elder brother down the stairs. I witnessed my father ruling the household and knew no other way of behaving. It was my responsibility to keep an eye on them and on this day Kevin was being a right little sod. I was cleaning the dining room table, a large wooden table which was divided into three sections. It had two hinges, one each end, so it could be folded down to make more room. Kevin kept putting his fingers in the hinge and I remember getting more and more cross. I said to him, 'If you put your finger in there again I'll chop it off'. Of course he kept his little finger in the gap and I pulled the leaf of the table up. As he yelped the top of his little finger stayed in the gap. 'Bloody great,' I thought, 'now I'll get a right telling off'. I don't remember if he went to hospital, but I suspect he probably did. He still shows me his little flat finger, and of course it taught him a lesson, he didn't do it again.

Actually this particular sibling was a bit accident prone. I remember another time when we had gone for a walk to the local lagoon. He had climbed up onto the edge where the water drained into a long sloping run away and had lost his footing and slipped into it. He sustained a nasty cut to his head. I managed to pull him out by his shirt, resulting in yet another trip to the hospital. I loved my younger brother dearly. He always seemed to get a raw deal from dad; in fact he was my father's punching bag on many occasions. I can vividly remember my father taking his belt to him on numerous occasions.

Arrested for Kung Fu Fighting

A neighbour knocked at our front door, she was in a panic and shouting at me 'Someone is beating your sister up'. I was fourteen years old at the time and over-protective towards my siblings. I immediately flew out of the front door and ran down the road. Diane was in the middle of a fight and she was definitely coming off worse. I grabbed the girl that was hitting her and remember wanting to kill her. I was like a mad person possessed. I couldn't stop hitting her – I punched, I kicked, I pulled her hair. Someone called the police fearful for the girl's life, and as soon as I heard this I ran home with Diane in tow. The police arrived at our house sometime later. I was shitting myself (well nearly), but I couldn't quite understand what I'd done wrong. I was summoned with my father to the police station. The other girl had been taken to hospital and was in a bit of a mess. I went with my father to meet Inspector Archer at the police station. She was horrid, but I was determined to not let it show that I was frightened of her. I gave her my account of what had happened and she said next time that I was to leave my sister to fight her own battles. She said she wanted an apology and the assurance it would not happen again.

I said, 'Why should I apologise, I've done nothing wrong?'

Her answer to me was, 'Apologise or stay all night'.

I flatly refused to apologise and I knew I was in for a long haul. At eleven p.m. and getting it in the neck from my father, I said I was sorry to the inspector and mumbled that it wouldn't happen again. On the way home my father said to me, 'Are you sorry?'

I replied, 'No and said I'd do the same again'.

The inspector said I'd have a criminal record until I was eighteen which was something I worried about for years.

Thinking back now I had so much anger inside of me the poor girl really didn't stand a chance.

Being Watched in the Bathroom

The bathroom door had been taken off its hinges and this was because dad liked to watch us in the bathroom. Initially we didn't have a shower just a bath. I would desperately try to put the door up in such a way that he couldn't see in, but because it wasn't on the hinges the door never quite stayed in place. Always a bloody gap, and a little voice inside my head saying, 'Always watching you!' I could hear dad breathing outside and sensed him watching me as I got undressed and washed myself. He was always bloody watching.

On Sunday evenings it was my job to bathe my siblings when they were small, all five together in the bath in barely enough water to cover their knees. They would sit one behind each other and each one washing the other's back. There was never much hot water so it was always used sparingly.

A short time before my father stopped sexually abusing my sister Diane, she was sitting in the bath and was by this time quite well developed. Father came into the bathroom without knocking as bold as brass. I turned to him and said, 'What do you think you're doing in here, you shouldn't be in here,' and to my surprise he turned round and left.

Diane left home shortly afterwards and many years later she told me she had had enough of cooking meals for people who didn't appreciate it. A brother had commented on a meal that she had prepared and that was the straw that broke the camel's back. She moved in with a family who lived in the same street as ours, only a few doors away. I didn't know until many years later that she was abused constantly day in day out by my father. When she reached the age of eighteen, she decided she couldn't take any more and left –no goodbyes, nothing. When I returned home to find her gone I was devastated. I went to see her, not to encourage her to come back, but to check that she was ok. She said nothing of her abuse and at this point my own abuse was so deeply buried in my unconscious I didn't make the connection. I knew I had to let her go but I felt as though I had lost a child and I wept and missed her dreadfully for weeks.

The couple who lived in the house where she went to live were and still are very special to her. They both cared for her deeply and looked after her unconditionally, treating her like their own.

While Diane was still living at home sometimes she would clean the ashes from the grate in the living room with the help of Iris, the lady with whom she went to live. She discussed with Iris how difficult it was to get the washing dry and hanging it in the airing cupboard upstairs sometimes helped. One day Iris followed Diane upstairs and, because the bedroom door was open, Iris could see the mattresses on the floor. She asked Diane where she slept and Diane replied, 'Over in the corner'. She asked Diane where the bedclothes were and Diane replied, 'I don't have any, just a coat to cover me'. Iris offered to purchase some pyjamas for her, but Diane asked if she could have a nightdress instead. Iris bought her a cream full-length nightdress with small red spots on it. Diane would wear it and Iris would wash it for her. Sometimes the nightdress would be soiled from urine from another family member who shared the same bed. Diane has never told them what happened to her in our house, but I'm sure they knew.

Nail, Neck and Bedroom Inspections

My father always insisted that all of his children had a weekly nail and neck inspection. This would be held in the living room or any room that he decided on. What a power crazed bastard he was. As children we would all queue up and hold out our hands, after which he would check our necks. If your nails were bitten or your neck was the slightest bit dirty, you were in the firing line. Actually it didn't matter even if your nails weren't bitten or your was neck dirty, it might be that you just weren't standing right or not looking at him, you could still get a good hiding. Damned if you did and damned if you didn't. If your neck was dirty you would be made to go and scrub it again and again, if he wasn't satisfied he would take over and scrub it until it bled. I never bit my nails but some of my siblings did and they would always get a good hiding, there was no escape. A verbal hiding would follow, or worse the belt or his fists. Every day in our house there were tears of some sort or other. When dad started shouting Wendy always attempted to get herself to the bathroom but usually she wet herself. Dad had a name for her 'piss pot'. Wendy remembers when her abuse stopped; she just doesn't remember when it started. Thank you Wendy for having the courage to speak out.

Another of my father's favourite routines was to hold bedroom inspections just like a sergeant major inspecting his barracks. If you knew an inspection was coming you could tidy your room as fast as humanly possible. We had so few possessions there was very little to tidy up, but I would always do my best to push my stuff under the bed, as far back as possible. If I was really lucky he wouldn't look under the bed.

If you had wet the bed, he would make you sit on the potty in the living room in front of everyone. I can only imagine the humiliation this would cause to my brothers and sisters. I certainly remember how I felt and that was just witnessing it. I certainly didn't want to watch. Sometimes he would insist that some of my siblings wore nappies and then he would make them sit or stand in the living room. My stomach would churn and I would feel physically sick just watching them endure their punishment. Some of us wet the bed some of us did not; luckily for me I didn't. Covers on the bed were a luxury which we didn't have. Most of the beds had newspaper to lie on and when this was urinated on it was disposed of, usually by being burnt. Some of my siblings smelt of stale urine, but of course it wasn't their fault. Old wet mattresses were stored in the loft and it stank up there. I remember burning the old stained newspaper in the garden and the smell of the stale, stinking smoke, slowly rising from a bonfire that didn't want to light. I wondered if the neighbours could smell it too and what they thought.

Another use for old newspapers was for Diane to be sick on after she'd been forced to perform oral sex on him. (*Bastard*) She was kept back from school and once we had left she had to do her duty and then she would be allowed to go to school. I wished she'd told me, I'd have murdered the bastard and gladly served time for it.

It wasn't unusual for us to get into trouble for the most menial things. If his shirt wasn't properly ironed, we would get a beating, despite the fact that the iron had broken ages ago.

To heat it up we needed to place it on the hot gas stove. Father would say, 'Who's done this? Who's done that?' We would then all be sent upstairs and told to decide amongst ourselves who was the culprit. As an adult I can see that it was all such a load of crap, actually he was such a bully and control freak. I can vividly remember thinking ok, who is going to own up to moving his newspaper or using the last of the shoe polish! On many occasions I said it was me, just to save the little ones from a senseless hiding.

Things that come to mind:

Cleaning out the grate for the fire
Polishing the hallway with dual cleaner. Having to scrape it off and redo.
No hoover, brushing the stairs.
No heating in the winter

The Clark Shoes – Tears on my Pillow

I desperately needed shoes. I usually had hand-me-downs that my older sister had grown out of but on this occasion I was going to be treated to a brand new pair. The other girls at school were wearing platforms and that was what I had my heart set on. My father had been saying for a while that I would have new shoes but definitely not platforms. I remember that I made such a fuss, saying I wouldn't wear flat shoes. My father teased me saying that's exactly what I would be getting. He said you will bloody well wear them even if I have to force you. The other threat was I could go to school with no shoes on. Maybe I should have done that!

The day came and my father and I walked into town to buy my shoes. He always walked really fast and I had to almost run to keep up with him. I still walk fast now and many people comment on it. We went into the Clarks shoe shop and I remember looking around for fashionable platformed shoes. There weren't any, just bloody awful sensible flat black and brown shoes. I didn't know where to look. I felt sure he wouldn't actually make me wear flat shoes. I made a scene in the shop saying I didn't want them. The lady came over to measure my feet; size six she told my father. This was the first time I'd ever been measured for shoes. She asked my father what shoes should she bring out for me to try and he pointed to the bloody flat ones. I felt sick and there was nothing I could do. The assistant went off and came back with the most hideous shoes I'd ever laid eyes on. The worst thing of all was they were brown! Dad was giving me such a glare, telling me what an ungrateful bitch I was. I did my best to pretend I couldn't walk in them, but to no avail the shoes came home with me, insistent all the way home that I would not wear them.

When we arrived home I was given such a hiding and sent to bed without having anything to eat. As for the shoes I shoved them as far back under my bed as I could, in the dark, out of sight and out of mind. My tummy churned.

In the morning the shoes stayed in the box under the bed while I got ready for school. The only pair of socks I possessed were barely dry and I put them on. I used to wash them out every day after school. Dad was waiting for me at the bottom of the stairs and asked where the shoes were. I replied bold as brass, 'I'm not going to wear them.'

I wasn't prepared for what followed. He just launched

himself at me, hitting me, swearing and shouting at the top of his voice. The final straw was a punch that landed square on the right side of my face. The power of the punch knocked me over and I was already bleeding from a cut on my head. It was at this point that I realised if I didn't get out right away there was every possibility he was going to kill me. I ran to the back door and out of the house. I turned left and hid in some bushes next to a row of garages and stayed there until I saw him leave for work. I knocked on the house at the end of our row and thankfully someone answered the door. A friend of mine Lorraine was still at home. She made me a cup of tea and I stayed there upset, bruised and battered for most of the day. We talked about reporting him to the police for what he'd done but I knew I couldn't do it – what could I do! I gave the shoes to my younger sister even though her feet were actually a size larger than mine. I kept out of his way for my own safety.

Child maltreatment, sometimes referred to as child abuse and neglect, includes all forms of physical and emotional ill-treatment, sexual abuse, neglect and exploitation that results in actual or potential harm to the child's health, development or dignity.

Statistics June 2012

A compilation of government, official, research and NSPCC statistics on child protection, safe-guarding and child abuse:

Approximately 50,500 children in the UK are known to be at risk of abuse right now.

One in four young adults (25.3%) were severely maltreated during childhood.

Sexual abuse
Nearly a quarter of young adults (24.1%) experienced sexual abuse (including contact and non-contact) by an adult or by a peer during childhood.

Physical violence
One in nine young adults (11.5%) had experienced severe physical violence during childhood at the hands of an adult.

Experiencing domestic abuse
Nearly one in four young adults (23.7%) were exposed to domestic violence between adults in their homes during childhood.

Bridge Over Troubled Water

Although I loved primary school, I hated secondary school. I disliked everything about it. Eight thirty and the never ending journey began to school which seemed like miles. I always knocked for the girl who lived in the house on the corner, despite the fact that her punches to my upper arms were never a welcome greeting. On cold frosty mornings my feet would hurt from the ill-fitting shoes given to me by my elder sister. I sometimes wore plimsolls instead of shoes and on wet mornings would cover each with a plastic bag to stop the rain from creeping in.

My uniform was always too small and in the summer months I'd be hot and sweaty because I never had deodorant.

I would sit in lessons and look out of the window, wishing I was somewhere else. I never liked the teachers and it always seemed that the clever children were the favourites. I loved to swim but hated changing in the communal changing room because my underwear was old, tatty and never fitted properly. I'm sure my breasts grew overnight, one day I didn't have any and the next day there they were. I always borrowed a swimming costume from close girlfriends because I didn't possess one of my own.

Children can be cruel and there were always comments thrown at me by my fellow classmates. I suppose you could call it bullying or was it simply the truth? The comments were usually about my mother's mental state, my clothes or the fact that there were so many children in our family. I would be asked if I was a Catholic or don't your parents have a television, but I never knew what to say in return. I missed so many schooldays taking turns with other siblings to care for my mother or younger siblings.

During classes I would spend my time looking out of the window and day dreaming. I didn't want to be at school but I didn't want to go home either. Walking to and from school I used to pass the different housing estates and I'd look into the windows and pretend I lived in the houses. I felt different from my friends but didn't understand quite what was different about me.

My favourite subjects were PE, Art, Physics and Biology and I decided I wanted to teach PE or join the army. My father had other ideas for me, however. He said the subjects I wanted to do were not fit for girls. He had already secured a job for my older sister and brother at ICI in Welwyn Garden City and he thought that I would naturally follow in their footsteps. The job he had chosen for me was an office job, but I hated the thought of being stuck indoors all day and flatly refused his offer. He told me I was an ungrateful cow.

I left school having passed all my exams and went to college to study commercial design. This lasted just a year because I couldn't afford to purchase all the equipment that I needed and consequently I fell behind. It was with regret that I left and I distinctly remember feeling that I was a failure. Most of the summer was spent looking after my younger siblings because of my mother's ill health. My father would tell me often that I was useless and no one would ever want to marry me. He would say he felt sorry for the poor bastard that ended up with me.

Friends

I had just a few friends, but dad's rule was none of them were allowed into our house. I didn't question this rule, I simply accepted it. No one questioned my father for fear of what would follow. If you did question his authority there would be hell to pay.

My best friend was Kim, she lived next door and we were friends from the day we moved to 56 in 1965. She lived with her three sisters, a brother and her parents. I loved to go into their house because they always had food. The cupboards and fridge were always full with all the things we didn't have. I never said anything about my own lack of food but my eyes would nearly pop out of my head from just looking at all the goodies they had. No wonder my father didn't want any of our friends coming into our house. We didn't have any food let alone a fridge. All we had was a large pantry in the kitchen which contained two shelves. Sometimes we had bread and there was usually a bag of sugar for my father's tea. I would sometimes catch my siblings eating the sugar by the spoonful. On odd occasions we would have strawberry jam; to this day I hate jam.

Other school friends of mine played an important part in my teenage years. Lorraine was not only a neighbour she was a pen friend and we wrote to each other for many years. She worked for The Royal Household Staff at Buckingham Palace in the dining room and I would eagerly await her letters on royal headed paper. I had an assortment of pen friends, a girl the same age as myself named Dianne in Canada, an army guy stationed in Germany and a boy from Korea who was learning to write English; his letters were sometimes hard to understand but they were always a joy to receive. Looking back now I think having pen friends was a line of communication to the outside world. This was a totally different world to 56. My pen friends were mine and mine alone. I kept my precious letters for many years and only recently have parted with a few.

Another friend of mine was Melanie, I think she lived with her grandparents or maybe it was an aunt. When my youngest brother was born she gave me a radio. I couldn't believe someone would give me such an expensive gift. The radio was purple and a heavy plastic with a big handle and I would listen to Radio Luxembourg during the night – I loved it – it was an escape from the world I had come to hate. At night I slept in the living room on the settee. When the baby woke for his night feed I would be so tired, the radio was a real comfort. Sometimes one of my sisters would also sleep downstairs. He was a good baby and didn't take too long after his feed to drift back off to sleep in his pram.

Mum looked ill most of the time which was another cause of my embarrassment. She didn't walk properly, her face would twitch and her hands moved in a most peculiar way. I feel sad now just thinking about her. I didn't understand what was wrong with her because she had acted this way for as long as I can remember. She had hardly any teeth and she didn't speak coherently; in fact if any words did come out of her mouth they usually were, 'Bloody kids, need them or fucking kids'. She would shout or mumble these words as she paced up and down the garden path. She too could be quite violent and would lash out at us without any warning. Most of the time I managed to keep out of her way but on occasions I would catch a smack across the face or legs. For the majority of the time her behaviour was like that of a child and, as the younger siblings got older if they were treated to sweets, I would always make sure she had some too.

As her illness got worse she became incontinent. She was still having periods and would sometimes soil herself. When she first became ill and I was able to care for her, my father had said it was our fault that she was like she was. He told us we would have to do everything for her which included feeding her, washing her and all the daily tasks that would make her life a little more comfortable. Other sisters took their turns at caring for her; some did a lot more than others. The boys seemed to be totally excluded from her daily care because in my father's words: 'its woman's work!'

Weekly Walks – Seasons in the Sun

On Sundays I would take the little ones (that's what I called them, an affectionate term) for a weekly walk. Some of them loved it some of them hated it. Strangely enough they nearly always came so it couldn't have been that bad. Dad would tell me to take them out and stay out which meant we could be gone for hours and sometimes all day. We would have nothing to eat or drink. Depending on the time of year sometimes we would find something to eat in the hedgerows, such as blackberries or fallen chestnuts in the woods. I knew exactly where to go. During the autumn we would go scrumping for apples. The house we went to for apples was massive with a huge garden that was situated near the Welwyn viaducts. The lady that lived there was old and was often out, so we took our chances. Unfortunately one day we did get caught taking already picked apples from inside the porch. They were in plastic bags on a shelf. She came out from the kitchen and we just stood there frozen to the spot from getting caught. I must have looked petrified and the old lady seemed sympathetic. She said we didn't need to pinch the apples we could help ourselves at anytime. I remember the apples were delicious – the tummy ache that followed was not so good.

The places I took the little ones to were places to escape from father – somewhere that he couldn't find us. This was a child's make-believe world of escapism. Sometimes we would be so tired we would find a suitable place to snooze.

One of my favourite places to take the little ones was the river Mimram in Welwyn. It was a place where you could be alone, where trees provided shade and shelter and the water was perfect to dip your toes on a hot day. I also would go there with my neighbour and friend Kim. We spent so many hours there together, much of the time in silence as we had an unspoken trust and understanding that we still have today. Even as children our unconscious minds worked together. Sometimes we did not need words, just a look, a touch or a smile. I took my siblings there often and we would play in the river catching crayfish and tiny sticklebacks, dipping our toes and feet in the icy cool water.

Sherrardswood was another destination as were the chalk pits, all places where we could just be children without fear of being reprimanded.

One weekly walk during the autumn we decided to collect some chestnuts. We would eat these raw and take some home to cook in front of an open fire. Diane had gone off to have a pee and a little while later had yelled out. I rushed to her to find her leg bleeding, just to the side of her left knee. She had caught herself on a barbed wire fence. The gash was particularly nasty and I knew that it would need stitches pretty quickly. I decided that she needed to go to hospital as soon as possible. I sent a brother to stop a car as we weren't too far from the road. No thought was given to the danger of accepting lifts from strangers and as luck would have it my brother flagged down a police car.

Diane and I travelled to the hospital in the back of the car, all the while I was thinking that my father was going to go ape shit. I'd sent the others home, telling them to be as quick as possible. Dad arrived at the hospital and played the caring father role. Diane had seven stitches on the inside of her leg and we went home.

Saddest Day

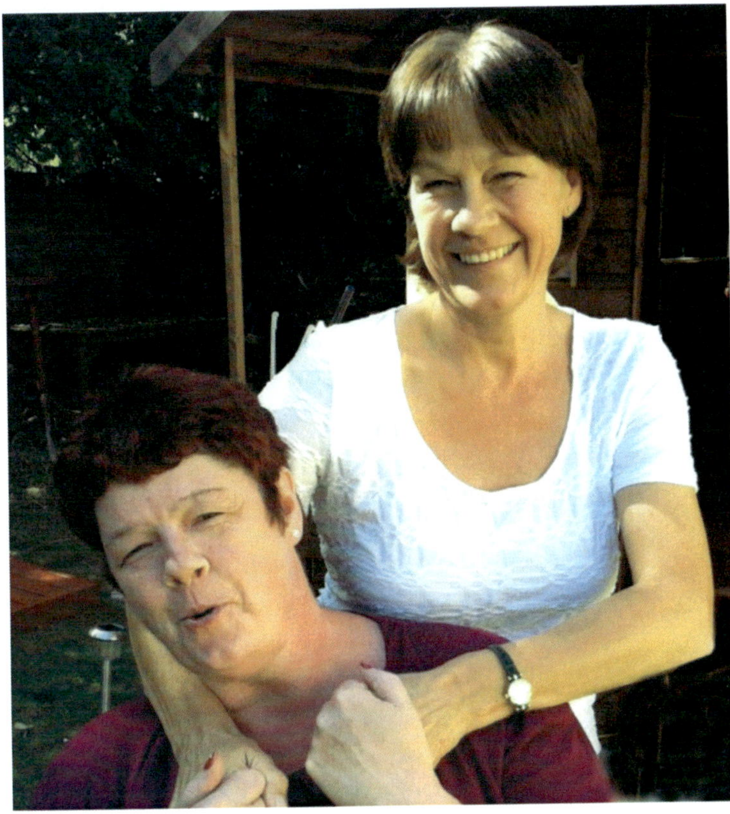

My sister Diane and me

When I was growing up I loved my sister Diane. She was a year younger than me and a quiet little girl. When we were teenagers, before she left home, she would cook, clean and take care of mum doing all the thankless tasks a child shouldn't have to endure. I had done the same, being a mother and a carer from such an early age. We both lost countless days from school and it hurts me still that I was not able to protect her more from the constant abuse. When my sister Diane and I were in our forties, she confided in me about a terrible thing that had happened to her as a young child. She was about six or seven years old and had been kept home from school as she wasn't feeling too well. My father came home most days for his lunch as he was working at ICI in Welwyn Garden City at the time. It took him approximately fifteen minutes to walk home. When he arrived there Diane was sitting on the settee opposite our mother. My father raped her while my mother sat reading the newspaper.

My father had a big, old, green photo album that he used to draw pictures in. He once sat me on his lap while we each took turns at drawing something for each letter of the alphabet. **I thought I was so lucky spending time with him**.

CHAPTER NINE

Returning Home

As an adult I would visit my parent's house as often as I could. On a fine summer's day during the school holidays I would travel with my son and daughter on the Green Line bus. We would walk the mile or so to the bus stop, armed with the buggy and various other things that we would need for our day out.

We arrived at my parents' house just before lunch. Mum had been eating a cream cake most of which was covering the bottom half of her face. She had no teeth just really hard gums. As her teeth began to decay over the years they fell out and an appointment was made for her to have them all removed. This operation was performed in hospital on September 21st 1979 and I was the one who signed the consent form, not my father. She had been losing her teeth due to the medication that she was taking. She was very unwell after initially having them all removed and I struggle now to try and understand why they were all removed at the same time. I have had the odd tooth extracted and know how much just having one out hurts, let alone all of them. The plan for her was to have a brand new set of dentures made. When the teeth were ready she had them fitted and they looked lovely. Unfortunately during a routine appointment with her physiatrist they were lost and it was suggested that she had accidentally flushed them down the toilet. Whenever I asked her about what had happened to her new teeth she would burst out laughing.

On this particular day she was enjoying a very large, fresh cream doughnut.

As I sat in the living room with my father sat opposite me, my daughter aged about three came into the room. I picked her up and sat her on my lap facing my father. I became increasingly aware he was looking at her, I watched him staring at my beautiful, innocent daughter as she kicked her legs to settle into a more comfortable position. Time stood still for me that day. The look on his face took my breath away. For a brief moment I was a little girl again and he was looking at me. The trigger inside was so intense I held my breath. I felt sick and nearly screamed out but managed to keep my composure. My father didn't notice me; he was trapped in his own sick world. At that moment I knew I would never under any circumstances leave any of my children with him. I didn't recognise at the time that this was what was occurring. Only years later would I make the sickening connection.

CHAPTER TEN

All About Mother

My mother for most of the time was mute and it doesn't matter how hard I try I cannot remember the sound of her voice. I can't be exactly sure when she stopped speaking, but I believe I was about eight or nine years old. Until I have access to her medical records I'll not know for sure.

So a silent mother I had. I did not understand what was wrong with her. She went to hospital on so many occasions not just to have babies, but for treatment for a mental illness. On her death certificate her cause of death is listed as:

1 (a) Congestive Cardiac Failure
   (b) Chronic Obstructive Pulmonary Disease

2 Chronic Schizophrenia

My mother had electric shock treatment in the 1960s/1970s and I can clearly remember an ambulance crew and a doctor turning up at the house to take her away. She would be on one side of the door crying, shouting while she was given an injection to calm her down and my father would be on the other side holding the door so she couldn't leave. I hated it, hated it all. I can recall even now one of the days she was taken away.

Lies and More Lies

May 5th 1971

Dear Dr Green

I was asked by Dr Watson to see this patient who I interviewed today having previously obtained her history from her husband last Friday.

I understand she is happily married with twelve children. Her husband is steadily employed with ICI. After the birth of her ninth child she indicated that she felt an old friend was in the house although there was, in fact, no one there and has continued to behave in a somewhat bizarre manner.

I understand she responded to the administration of Moditen tablets prescribed by you.

When I saw her today she showed no florid symptoms but did not have complete insight into her abnormal behaviour in the past. I think her symptoms are indicative of schizophrenic illness and feel she would benefit from phenothiasines. I would suggest Stelazine 10mg b.d but Moditen could be equally well used if you prefer this.

It is clear she should not have any more children but has refused to be sterilised. Her husband is agreeable, however, to have a sterilisation operation and she did not object to this action when I discussed this with her today.

Yours sincerely
J.L.McClure
Consultant Psychiatrist

August 7th 1972

Dear Dr Watson

This patient, much to her surprise, finds herself in her 10th or 11th pregnancy. She does not know how and refuses to admit that this is true. She thinks her last period was some time in January and I found her uterus at the 32-week level.

After her 8th pregnancy she had a psychotic breakdown which I dealt with at home and since then she has continued to have delusional ideas. It appears she does not want the babies but likes being pregnant.

You will have her obstetric history. The reason I referred her for a special appointment rather than a routine booking is because of the great difficulty in getting her near a hospital at all. When I saw her last week she complained that she nearly fainted and I fear that her haemoglobin has fallen. I am trying to encourage her to take some iron tablets and also Moditen to relieve her tensions. I have arranged for my Health Visitor to escort her to your clinic to make sure she attends. I am willing to do her antenatal routine visits at her home if you think this is easier than getting Mrs Arm for her appointment. I feel she must be delivered in hospital.

Yours sincerely,

R. Cope

P. Watson, Esq., F.R.C.S., F.R.C.O.G.

Queen Elizabeth 11 Hospital

Part letter written by my father to Dr Green

February 7th 1974

Dear Dr Green,
I must apologise for writing to you instead of making an appointment but I felt it easier to remember everything by writing.

I have recently discovered, regretfully, that my wife is some 6-7 months pregnant, a fact which had gone unnoticed mainly because we both have very little contact with each other.

Over the last year my wife's mental condition has changed little, which, because of her attitude to almost everything, makes it hard for me to understand how she has become pregnant. ***(Because, you raped her daddy dear!)***

March 21st 1974

Mother is sectioned under the Mental Health Act 1959–25

I remember the day like it was yesterday…

The ambulance arrived. Two men came to the door accompanied by the social worker and they were led into the house by my father. Mother was in the living room hiding behind the door and clearly very frightened about what was about to happen to her. I didn't know what to do, so I just watched.

I can hear her now as she clung onto the door, screaming,

crying 'No, no!' desperately trying to pull the door open to make her escape. Father held the door on the other side so that she couldn't get out. The men went around the other way to administer the injection that would leave her submissive and without the will to fight … in other words to make it easier for them to take my mum away again. I am helpless and I do not fully understand what is playing out before my very eyes. Then they are all gone … I am just fifteen years old, lost, empty and all alone. I knew the little ones needed collecting from school, so once again I have to wear a brave face.

She was sectioned under the Mental Health Act of 1959–25 and arrived at the hospital at 2.45 p.m.

> Mrs Arm has 11 children at home age ranging from 17 years to 18 months and is approximately 8 months pregnant. Arrangements for the care of the children have been seen to by Mr Arm – at least for the next week or so.

(I think that should say, arrangements for the care of the children will be myself and other siblings)

Reason for admission

She was admitted under Section 25 having been seen by Dr Gander an emergency domiciliary. She was described as being aggressive and that she had attacked a social worker just prior to admission. She was also described as being psychotic due to the fact that she refused to admit to being pregnant when this was very obvious. Dr Gander felt that she had an incongruous affect and was thought-disordered.

On examination

To Dr D. R. Gander

She appeared as an obese woman, usually sitting by herself in the ward never noted to ever talk to other patients. Wearing dark glasses 'because my husband gave them to me' and speaking in a monotone way with a high-pitched voice. Conversation was inappropriate and vague, appeared somewhat bewildered. No delusions were expressed and she accepted the reality of her baby. She showed schizophrenic thought disorder.

The day following her admission she went into labour refusing to believe pregnancy, even when her membranes ruptured. Delivery was uneventful, assisted breech. Her husband proved to be a very odd person in that he was continually telephoning, asking numerous questions regarding her management, medication etc. Apparently he kept a graph of her mood state. He appeared to show no anxiety and was quite confident to speak in front of a ward round, to Dr Gander, assuming the interviewer's role. Patient's mental state changed very little during her stay and eventually she discharged herself on termination of Section 25 with the agreement of her husband.

Discussions with husband – attempts were made to encourage both sterilisation of his wife and his own sterilisation by vasectomy. However, these suggestions were rejected and she returned home, no doubt to continue her breeding behaviour.

P. M. Graham
Registrar in psychiatry

Nurses Notes

June 22nd 1978
Termination of pregnancy at 16 weeks.

June 27th 1978
Referred back from Codicote ward following T.O.P and also sterilisation.

June 30th 1978
Doreen kept wandering back to ward, unable to concentrate. Sleeping well. Sees all, hears all and says nothing.

July 4th 1978
Husband seen by Dr Gander decided to continue Stelazine medication for further period.

Mr Arm refused to have Doreen home for the weekend. Very reluctant to help her in any way.

July 6th 1978
She fell going down some stairs; right ankle is hurting, no swelling or bruises. Observe.

July 7th 1978
Doreen went to church. Bought up to ward by husband saying his wife had slipped again and bruised her knee and her ankle is hurting. Bruise cleaned and plaster applied to ankle. Pain killer to be given if she complains.

July 8th 1978
Usual wandering around aimlessly. Still attempting to put herself to bed during the day. Continues to appear vague, muddled and confused. Visited by her family.

July 11th 1978
Home for the weekend.

Discharged on 21st July 1978 back home (*house of horrors*).

August 17th 1978
Family say they expected her to be better after her stay in hospital. They are all very concerned about the younger children who have to be cared for by the older children. Diane (18 years) is at home at present. Doreen takes no interest at all and spends most days in bed.

August 25th 1978
Visited family and met the smaller children who are delightful and well behaved. The older members do a fine job.

September 18th 1978
She did not attend the outpatients on Friday. Family say she shouts in the house, bangs doors and even shouts in the street. Family have acquired an Alsatian bitch – ex police dog.

November 7th 1978
Phone call from a neighbour who was worried about Diane.

February 27th 1979
Called to visit family, apparently Diane has left to live with a friend.

The following comment was written in mum's outpatient notes on September 17th 1980:

> 'Remains well, but nutty as a fruit cake.'

I cried when I read this, my lovely mum, through no fault of her own, being described by someone as being 'as nutty as a fruit cake'!

Visiting Mum in Hospital

When I was older I visited my mother on a secure locked ward at the local hospital, my elder brother came too. I remember that we had to wait to be let in. The door was unlocked then locked securely behind us by a nurse who told us to follow her to the ward. There were a lot of patients on that ward, some just sitting, staring, others were watching television but without really taking in what they were watching. Mum was in a chair just sitting. She looked lonely and I felt terribly lost. I remember thinking, 'Why can't I just have a normal mum'. I looked into her eyes, held her hand and just wished she would speak to me, even a single word so that I knew my mother was somewhere inside that vacant stare.

I visited her on my own on a few occasions and during one of these visits we sat together and I asked her how she was. She looked straight at me and said, 'I don't know what I'm doing in here, they're all bloody mad'. I nearly fell off the chair. I thought, 'Oh my god she's ok, she can speak'. This was one of the only times I've felt there was any hope! When she came back home after more treatment she seemed fine for about a week. I believe she had received electric shock treatment and this was confirmed many years later during a meeting with one of her physiatrists and her sister Grace who had worked at the hospital for twenty-three years. It was this aunty who visited my mother daily whenever she was an inpatient. After a few days my mother became mute again. Dad would spend his time shouting, angry and having a go at her and us every day. During one of these violent phases I was upstairs in my room when mum came in and sat on my bed. I held her hand tightly. I had a bunk bed at this time and slept on the upper bunk. He stormed into the room and was shouting, saying how fucking useless we were. He put his face close to my mother's and told her she was fucking mad and that it was entirely my fault she was like she was. He started to lash out at her, throwing his fists. I was in front of her trying to protect her from the punches, almost lying on top of her. I didn't want him to hit her; all I knew was that she needed protecting. Even though I was petrified of what was happening I knew I could not let him hit her, she was just too vulnerable. I took the full force of his attack and had the cuts and bruises to show for it. Even to this very day I don't know why I never said anything to anybody. I was so scared every bloody day of my life – so scared.

Mother was raped by my father day in and day out. I could here him in their bedroom, shouting at her to shut up. I vividly remember when I was very little hearing her on many occasions crying and she would say, 'Please Geoff, no stop', but of course he never did. There were days when she would be bruised on her face and arms. When her condition had deteriorated and she needed help in the bathroom, I often noticed bruising on the tops of her inner thighs. I didn't make the connection then that he was raping her. She was a defenceless woman, helpless against his brutal attacks.

August 1st 1989 Letter regarding mum

Letter written by Dr R. Hanak
Locum SHO to Dr Leon Gittelson

> Dear Gill
>
> Re: Mrs Doreen Arm – dob 11–10–1935
>
> Doreen is a chronic schizophrenic lady who has been attending the day hospital for many years. She currently attends on Tuesdays and Fridays. Her condition has been stable for a long time and she is not gaining anything from day hospital attendance apart from two days away from her husband. Mr Arm is known to abuse alcohol and to have a violent temper. For a long time there have been suspicions that he abused his wife physically. Last week one of her daughters rang the day hospital and spoke to the nursing staff. She was very distressed and frightened and reported that Mr Arm had been physically abusive to Doreen again. All the children are terrified of their father and the daughter begged that we would not tell the father that she had phoned. There were no apparent injuries on Doreen.

I do not know how we can help this lady, but feel we must not ignore these warning signs. She is clearly at risk of abuse and cannot tell us what is happening. I wonder whether one of your departments could visit her at home to pick up any further clues and to interview her husband on how well he is coping with looking after her. If you have any ideas for helping us to protect Doreen I would be grateful to hear them.

Yours sincerely
Dr B.Hanak

September 25th 1990

Letter written by Dr Leon Gittelson
Locum Consultant Psychiatrist

Dear Dr Green,
I saw several daughters of Mrs Arm and also Mrs Arm's sister, together with Mrs Arm's CPN, Peter Ormerod, in my out-patients clinic on the 18th September.

The reason for the consultation was that the family are concerned that Mr Arm is physically abusing his wife. There was also some possibility of emotional and even sexual abuse being mentioned.

There was a particular question as to whether it might be appropriate to use the Mental Health Act to bring Mrs Arm into hospital for her own safety and my view was that this was not the case. I also consulted with the duty Social Worker at Hatfield, Stella Loved, who also felt that, after consultation with her team, this would not be the right approach. It seems that we have here a lady whose main problem is that she has been physically abused by her husband and that the correct route towards getting help for her would be for the family to inform the police that this is taking place. Naturally they were reluctant to do this and the matter is still being considered by the family with regard to what possible options they have available to them.

I have not arranged to see the family again, at the present time, but the matter has been left in the hands of the CPN Mr. Peter Ormerod.

This letter is one of many, a cry for help, once again not heard.

December 5th 1990

Letter from Dr Hameen Markar MRCP MRC Psych

Re: Mrs Doreen Arm – d.o.b. 11.10.1935

Your mother, Mrs Arm, suffers from a chronic psychotic illness which is probably schizophrenic in nature. When she first presented to this hospital she had a number of acute schizophrenic symptoms. Over the years, these have become less severe and she now has what we call a defect state – in other words a burnt out illness. It is unlikely that she would improve any further and our aim is to maintain her in the present state for as long as possible.

If you need any other information please do not hesitate to contact me.

Days out shopping with mum

Once I'd left home, my other sisters and myself would take mother out shopping. These trips for me were always sad as they just highlighted the fact that she was so dependant and that I didn't have a proper mother. I believe she enjoyed them although I can never be certain. My elder brother and I were in charge of her accounts and whenever she needed anything, the rule was always no expense spared. She always had the best shoes and clothes, things that had been denied to her when we were children. Mum would sit in her wheelchair as we pushed her around. She would stretch her arms out to touch the clothes in the ladies department of Marks & Spencer and John Lewis and we would jokingly say to her, 'What would you like? Have anything'. She always had something. Sometimes we would stop for cake and a cup of tea. This was always difficult because she never really drank the tea. She would bring the cup up to her lips but not take any into her mouth, most would spill or the small amount she did manage to get into her mouth would dribble out. She always ate with her fingers never using a knife, fork or spoon.

Wednesday, October 26th 2011

Yesterday I received a phone call from Sandra Carter, a Mental Health Senior Care Records Administrator, regarding my mother's hospital notes and they are arriving tomorrow. My tummy is churning. I did not sleep well last night in anticipation of the notes arriving. The post came at ten o'clock and I could tell straight away the envelope was thin … my heart sank. I had waited five weeks for this day. I opened the letter and inside was about ten pages of copies of appointments from the late 1990s, details that I already held. Once my frustration, disappointment and anger had subsided I rang Sandra Carter and explained that the doctor had said I could have copies of all her medical notes and that I couldn't understand why I had only received the ten copies. I now have to wait another week as the secretary is on annual leave. Bloody great. I hope this is just a minor hiccup.

I have spoken to Sandra Carter again and it is now Wednesday, 2nd November. She said that she will telephone Mr Singh's secretary for me. Sandra says Dr Singh has said he will not give permission for me to have any other Doctors correspondence contained in my mothers notes, because some of them have passed away!! I rang Tanya his secretary and explained about our meeting and that he had said I could have copies of all her notes, so I couldn't understand why I he had changed his mind. She said she will speak to him later and find out the reason. I have also asked if I could sit with the notes at the hospital and just read them. I am cross, frustrated, upset, angry and my face is numb. I must calm myself down before I go off to work. If he has made his decision then I'm not sure where I go from here. Tanya said I probably shouldn't have been given access to her GP notes. Well just as bloody well I have them.

Thursday 8th December

Today I await the arrival of my mother's mental health records after a phone call yesterday from Sandra Carter. I feel slightly nervous at the prospect of what I might discover. I am still waiting for news of the rest of her general hospital records.

CHAPTER ELEVEN

1978

Tuesday, 13th June 1978

Dr Gander came to our house said mum has to go back to hospital.

Sunday, 16th July 1978

Mum kicked up quite a fuss about going back to hospital.

Take a Chance on Me

In September 1977 I had my first full-time job working at the QE2 Hospital in Welwyn Garden City, I was eighteen years old. I was fortunate to get the job as it had been turned down by the previous applicant. I worked as a sterile products assistant in the pharmacy and I loved it because it made me feel important. This was the first time I'd actually felt like I belonged somewhere. In January 1978 I first met my husband to be. He was a pre-registration student from Chelsea University and was studying Pharmacy. At first I didn't pay much attention to him because the students were a bit of a pain. I use to show them how to seal ampoules with the hot flame of a bunsen burner but as soon as they knew enough to be of any use to us, they would be gone. Neil had been warned about me, my boss had said I was a bit of a live wire and he should be careful what he said to me. (*Charming*)

In early June 1978 I arrived home from work feeling tired and hot. My feet hurt from the long walk home and they were smelly as I kicked my shoes off. I'd only been home a short while and my father was standing in the living room and looking somewhat fidgety. He said Tracey (his bit on the side) would be ringing shortly to speak to me. I thought, great what does the silly cow want me for, and shortly afterwards the telephone rang in the hall. My father answered it and called me over. I wasn't in any hurry to talk to her so I took my time, much to the annoyance of my father I'm sure. I took the bright red receiver from my father, sat down on the seat and listened to what she had to say. She said she was sorry to give me such sad news over the phone, but she thought it would be easier than my father telling me. I think there's a joke there somewhere. I was only half paying attention to her quietly spoken words, 'Your mother has cancer'.

I asked her, 'Cancer, where?' I said.

I was totally shocked and unprepared for this news. I felt sick and it was just as well I was sitting down. I looked up for my father but he wasn't there. What a bloody coward he was, why couldn't he tell me himself.

On the other end of the line a reply came, 'The cancer is in her stomach'.

Some of my siblings had been given the news earlier by my father.

On Monday, June 19th 1978, mother was taken to hospital by one of our neighbours named Iris. She would be having a procedure on the June 22nd. I worked at the same hospital and I remember asking my boss if I could visit my mother on the ward. My boss was a kindly man and was more than happy for me to go.

She had been admitted first to the Psychiatric ward and then transferred to Codicote ward, which I found with ease. I was fit and well and ran up the worn wooden stairs missing a few steps now and again. I knew my way around the departments now. The ward was bright, clinical and had a distinct smell of overcooked cabbage and urine that hung in the air. Mum was next to the window in a bay with three other ladies. She looked tired and frail in between the starched covers. She rarely spoke.

I said 'Hi' and kissed her cheek, asking her if she wanted anything. I was totally shocked when she whispered 'water'.

'Ok,' I said and went off to ask the nurse if I could get her a drink of water. The nurse replied a little brusquely, 'No, she can't have any before her surgery'. Her comment made me feel stupid and embarrassed, but I managed to pluck up the courage to ask her what sort of surgery she was going to have. The nurse's demeanour changed and she looked at me sympathetically and replied, 'A termination and sterilisation'.

I tried to look as normal as possible. I couldn't quite believe what I was hearing and asked how many weeks pregnant she was. The nurse said, 'Sixteen weeks'.

I was confused by this answer and I turned and went to sit with my mother. I looked at her, held her hand and told her she could have some water later. Looking out of the window I could see the trees opposite and the colour of the leaves beginning to darken. I thought how strange time was and the ever-changing seasons; mother now in her autumn years and me in spring. I felt lost, angry and sick but didn't want show to it. She was pregnant again! The thought kept going round and round in my head. The only blessing was she would finally be sterilised, it could never happen again. I eventually had to leave her to return to work. So father had lied again – no surprises there – she didn't have cancer she was actually pregnant with her fifteenth child.

According to records that I later found...

For the next hour I sat with Neil in the canteen and poured my heart out to him. He provided me with hot cups of tea and a listening ear. It was during this time that I started to realise that he was special. He was a lot taller than me at over six feet, with the loveliest big, blue eyes. From that day on he always made time to enquire as to how I was. He would tap on the glass door with his long black umbrella as he was leaving in the evening. I loved it and I knew I was falling in love with him. Life back home was horrid but going to work was an escape and seemed almost normal.

It wasn't until a few months later when Neil was due to leave that I realised I didn't even have his phone number or address. Outside of work I would cycle when the opportunity arose. I had bought a bike from Halfords and paid for it by monthly instalments. With the help of my sister Mandy, we planned to find out where Neil lived. We cycled to the nearest phone box and with a list of all the 'Sparrows' surnames in Stevenage in front of us, started to phone each and every one. In turn I asked to speak to Neil and on the third attempt I hit the jackpot, a man answered the phone and said, 'Hang on I'll get him'. I replaced the receiver as quickly as possible which made my sister and I laugh like silly school children. I now had his address and phone number. What I was going to do with it, I had no idea? We both giggled.

When we arrived back home we were questioned by my father as he wanted to know where we'd been and what had we been up to. He was such a control freak, so we told him we had just been out for a cycle ride, nowhere in particular.

As the time approached for Neil to finish at the hospital, a leaving do was arranged at the local pub called the Beehive. I went with a few work colleagues and watched and waited. I was thinking I might never see Neil again and felt quite sad at the thought. I was feeling quite desperate about seeing him again when I received an invite to another joint party – I was so happy.

The party was noisy with lots of alcohol flowing and Neil and I started talking about family and work. I'd had quite a lot to drink and remember feeling really happy. Neil needed the loo and for some reason I followed him. I could see the surprised look on his face when he realised I was behind him in the bathroom. He asked me to hold his beer while he took a wee. Of course I said 'Yes'. While he was going to the loo I plucked up the courage to ask him to marry me! To my complete surprise he said YES.

CHAPTER TWELVE

Together We Are Beautiful

The following February, on the 18th to be precise, Neil and I got engaged. The ring had been chosen by me from Godshaws in Welwyn Garden City. It was my ring and I wasn't going to have anyone else choose it. It was perfect, with two diamonds and a beautiful sapphire and I felt that I was the luckiest girl in the world.

We were married the following April in St Mary's Church, Digswell. I had wanted all my sisters as bridesmaids, sadly this wasn't to be. I had only four in the end – Sharon, Sarah, Sandra and Penny. They all looked beautiful and innocent, but looking back now at the photographs I can see a sadness in some of their faces. This was not only the happiest day, but also one of the saddest days of my life. My father was drunk and I held him up as we walked down the isle. Diane was not at our wedding as she had already left home. My father had made his feelings quite clear and had banned her from attending. Later in the day Neil and I had taken her some cake and I gave her an enormous hug. We were preparing to leave the house where our reception had been held, when I noticed five of my younger siblings sitting on the stairs, some together some on their own. The youngest of all said through tears, 'She's coming back you know'.

Those words broke my heart, but I couldn't cry just yet, that would have to wait. Leaving those little children was one of the hardest things I have ever had to do. I felt like a mother abandoning her children and I was torn in two and deeply distressed. I cried myself to sleep that night, hiding under the covers with my new husband lying beside me, totally unaware of my grief.

Our week's honeymoon was spent in Lyme Regis, Dorset. We stayed at the High Cliff Hotel and it was perfect; we walked, we ate and we made love. For the time being I put No. 56 to the back of my mind. I remember that Mandy had lent me a purple cardigan and I wore it nearly everyday.

Our newly married life started in a three bedroomed council property in Shepall in Stevenage. The house and garden was a mess and needed a lot of maintenance. In fact the whole property had been left in an incredible state by the previous owners, with dark brown paintwork and yellow ceilings. The bathroom had black/grey tiles and the walls were a cherry pink colour. That didn't stop us though, it was our first home and we spent many hours changing it to a style that suited us. I did the wallpapering and we shared the painting. I actually loved to decorate and changed the decor often. Neil would often go to work and come home to find the colour had been changed yet again.

Our life was hectic and I was always busy doing something. Weekends usually consisted of visits from family or friends. Some weekends Neil worked with his father in the local chemist, or did overtime at his usual place of work.

August 27th 1980

Today I did a pregnancy test and it was positive I weigh 8st 12lb and I'm very happy about that.

November 26th 1980
Had my scan at 9.30 – just one baby.

November 29th 1980
Took dad to do his Christmas shopping and he stinks of booze.

December 25th 1980
Stayed last night at mum and dads. Cooked Christmas lunch and we all sat down together. I'm 23 weeks pregnant.

April 23rd 1981
Nobody told me it would be like this. What has happened to my tummy? As I sit in an enormous, white, cold enamel bath with three inches of salty water covering my stitched bits I cry. I stay in the hospital for five days because that's just what new mums did in the eighties. I do my post natal exercises everyday; I will fit back into my jeans even if it kills me. I don't need to learn all this stuff about caring for a new baby, I already know it. What I didn't know was the changes that would happen to my twenty-two-year-old body now that will take time to get use to.

I return home a week later with my new baby boy. The first nappy change is a memorable one. The living room carpet is awash with an assortment of baby products, terry nappies, baby lotion, cotton wool, nappy pins and of course our baby. Neil and I look at each other and look at the carpet covered in baby products. How can such a tiny thing need so much stuff?

Welcome home Graham.

May 18th 1981

I stand holding my new baby son and I'm lost in my thoughts as I stare out the window at the blue sky. I cradle him in my arms and I sing to him with a heart so full of love that I'm sure it will burst. I sing the songs from the Carpenter's and rock him gently back and forth.

On the day that you were born,
The angels got together
And decided to create a dream come true
So they sprinkled moon dust in your hair of gold
and starlight in your eyes of blue

My first born son was and is a joy. From the moment he was born I have loved him unconditionally. Isn't that what mothers are supposed to do? I wonder if my mother ever sang to me…

May 1st 1982

Graham has taken his first step.

August 13th 1982

Neil burned both his hands and arms at work. Neil's dad was sacked from his job; Mary says we can't tell anyone about it. I hate secrets.

August 15th 1982

I showered Neil and washed his hair, his burns are not as red today.

My father would sometimes come over on his motorbike to borrow money, which he nearly always paid back. I made a point of not letting him smoke in my house, something that irritated him. My siblings would take turns to come and stay during school holidays, this was something I always enjoyed, as it made me feel I was doing my bit towards looking after them. I would often buy my younger siblings clothes from my catalogue and feed them tasty, hearty meals. The two youngest boys came to stay when our youngest son was about three years old. We visited my husband's parents and stayed for a drink and biscuits. When my husband's mother was passing the biscuit tin to the boys, my youngest brother looked up at her and said, 'No creams?' We did laugh and still do to this day.

The years that followed were happy and sad. I always felt that something wasn't quite right and that a part of my life was missing, I just couldn't put my finger on it and pushed the thought to the back of my mind. On one occasion my husband and I had picked up my two youngest brothers from my parents' house. We walked the mile or so to the railway station and as we approached a grassy area both boys ran off as if unleashed for the first time. My husband just stared at them and said it was like watching two dogs loose, both going in opposite directions. I loved having them to stay and they were great company for our son because the age gap was very close. I shudder now thinking of the girls left behind and what may have taken place.

August 16th 1982

I took the boys home and Penny came back to stay for a few days. Neil had his bandages changed.

August 23rd 1982
Take Penny home and bring Sandra back to stay.

October 9th 1982
Neil fainted this morning in the shower, that's not right and he really shouldn't go to work but we need the extra money.

October 11th 1982
Neil very unwell so called the doctor, who then came to see him. His temperature was 103. A urine sample was taken and the doctor thinks he has a virus.

It turns out Neil has jaundice and a liver infection; I'm not feeling very well either.

Neil has to go to the hospital for further tests.

I'm starting to go yellow and my wee stinks. I have no energy.

October 21st 1982
We both have Hepatitis. Probably caught from a dodgy piece of fish from a fish and chip shop during our holiday in Pevensey in August.

I have to go to hospital for further tests. The doctor said only half my liver is working. We both have to have fat-free diets, no alcohol for six months and Neil has been signed off for a further six weeks. Thank goodness Graham is okay.

Time waits for no man…

March 2nd 1984
Finally plucked up the courage to go to the doctors, mainly because of the recent miscarriage and the fact we have been

trying for another baby for some months now. Apparently I have a retroverted uterus which means it tilts backwards.

March 10th 1984
Ordered some clothes for Lawrence and Adam from my catalogue.

March 12th 1984
Dad came over and I lent him ten pounds. He said the poodle had died and he'd buried it in the garden. He said with no emotion at all that he had given it some of mum's medication. Bloody hell I'm sure that's not right.

22nd March 22nd 1984
The boys were very happy with their new clothes.

April 4th 1984
Washing blowing on the line, Graham playing in the mud with the worms and ladybirds. Such a joy just watching my little boy grow up.

April 7th 1984
Today I feel sad and fed up; I'm wondering what it would be like to have a mother to talk to?

April 11th 1984
Stayed a few days at Sharon's, did her ironing and helped with her new baby. I've been married for four years and it feels like forty. My period hasn't started.

April 14th 1984

Today I did a pregnancy test which was positive. I've cleaned the kitchen, hung the washing out and vacuumed. Neil seems happy.

April 23rd 1984

Happy third birthday Graham. Neil passed his driving test.

Morning sickness that lasts all day, bloody great it must be a girl, interfering with my hormones.

May 15th 1984

Doctor's appointment at 16.05 the doctor said I didn't feel nine weeks pregnant, also I'm more likely to miscarry because of my retroverted uterus. Thanks a bunch… He has advised me to lay on my tummy twice a day for ten minuets.

May 25th 1984

Scan and all is well, baby due December 19th. Still feeling sick for most of the day.

September 7th 1984

Baby kicking like mad, yes I know you are there. Diane telephoned and told me she is expecting a baby next May.

September 13th 1984

Go to mum and dad's today. The doctor is coming to see mum regarding an attendance allowance claim form. Their house is such a depressing place; I love my mum and wish she was well.

September 22nd 1984
I can hardly walk because my back is so sore.

September 26th 1984
Our little boy decided to water the carpets upstairs and the stair carpet. Neil and I could hear his footsteps running back and forth across the landing. When I went to investigate what was going on I watched him without him knowing, he was running back and forth to the bathroom filling a plastic container with water and throwing the water in every direction. When I asked him what he was doing he simply said, 'watering the carpet'. I hid my smiles and told him that only the grass needed watering not carpets.

October 6th 1884
One year since my miscarriage.

December 3rd 1984
No stretch marks.

December 11th 1984
Having our new bedroom carpet fitted today. I have moved the bed and cupboards out. When the guys came to fit the new carpet I joked with them saying that I was in labour. I've never seen a carpet laid so quickly.

I've had a show and my labour started at about 7 pm. The ambulance arrived at 12.30 pm... The driver and assistant both smelt of alcohol. 'Merry Christmas,' they said. Neil and I exchange glances. My contractions are every ten minutes and they hurt.

In the hospital a nurse straps a monitor to my belly and Neil and I watch the heart rate of our baby. The heart beat registers one hundred and sixty beats per minute. I know it's a girl. The lady in the room next to us sucks in her gas and air and sounds like a cow. Flipping heck do I have to put up with that all night. YES…

My baby is lying with it's spine to my spine… back ache labour, a little different to last time.

At 06.53 our little girl makes her grand entry into our world, she takes her first breath as I hold mine waiting for her cry… she has a good pair of lungs and lots of dark hair.

Hazels birth 12th December 1984

Isn't she lovely
Isn't she wonderful
Isn't she precious
Less than one minute old
I never thought through love we'd be
Making one as lovely as she
But isn't she lovely, made from love

12th December 1984
The hospitals heating has broken and we are told to take our precious bundle home.

I am as happy as happy can be. The house is filled with pink things. A sister for Graham and a daughter for Neil. We are blessed.

The day three blues come and my tears fall.
Exercise, exercise, exercise got to get those jeans on.

*****

July 6th 1987
We moved from Stevenage to our new home in St Neots, Cambridgeshire.

August 1st 1987
Bought a swing and slide for Graham and Hazel they both love it.

August 3rd 1987
Sharon, Derek and their girls move into the house next door. How cool is that, my sister living next door.

August 6th 1987
Dad said he'd given up drinking (*no such luck*) the children all seem well and mum smiled a lot today. I love my family.

August 8th 1987
Today we got a kitten for Graham and Hazel.

August 14th 1987
Looking after Hayley and Natalie all day.

October 31st 1987
Had my hair permed, not as pleased as last time. Neil collects his new car. Nova 1.3 silver.

Church service and Sunday school, dear God please make my mum better.

November 4th 1987
Why haven't I come on?

Friday
Thank goodness I've started my period.

November 8th 1987
Period didn't really start, shit I wonder if I'm pregnant, what am I going to tell Neil.

November 9th 1987
Waited for most of the day, I decided to walk to town to buy a pregnancy test. All I need to do is wait, then I'll know one way or another, the test was positive.

I really wasn't expecting this… what do they say 'play with fire and you'll get burnt'

June 30th 1988
Collected pram from Cambridge and its beautiful, navy cord silver cross. Cost £124.00

July 1st 1988
My brother Kevin going into hospital, having his appendix out tomorrow.

Sunday, July 3rd 1988
Visited Kevin in hospital he looks well and I'm fat.

Wednesday, July 6th 1988
One year since we moved from Stevenage to St Neots. I've had

a show at 07.30. A friend has offered to take care of Graham and Hazel.

Neil and I make the twenty-minute journey to the hospital. I'm in labour and have had contractions on and off all day. This baby is taking its time.

Have eaten too many Mars Bars and walked too many miles in the never-ending corridors of Hinchingbrooke hospital.

The night staff arrived at nine o'clock and they decided to put a drip up and administer some oxytocin, they say that should get things going. They were right of course within twenty minuets my contractions are more painful, I can't walk around because I'm strapped to a monitor and a drip. I don't like this feeling of helplessness. I need to take control and concentrate on my breathing. The gas and air are wonderful.

Our beautiful baby boy has arrived at 11.56 weighing 7lb 4oz. I feel amazing and full of energy. Tomorrow I shall go home with my new baby son with no name.

July 8th 1988

Today I am upset, different people keep knocking on the front door, I wish they'd all go away. The after pains are really painful.

July 12th 1988

The midwife came; she said I should lie on my tummy as my uterus is not going back as well as it should. We have named our little baby Geoffrey and he is beautiful. I want my dad to be proud of me that's why we've named him Geoffrey.

The hours, the days and weeks pass by and our little boy is sick. He is pale and has a troubled look on his perfect face.

After numerous trips to the doctors and hospital we discover he is allergic to cow's milk. A diet of soya milk and exclusion of lactose will help the paediatrician says.

For now the sickness stops and we are relieved. We are told he will grow out of it, I do hope so.

It's three am, they're all asleep, and no one is here to see.
As we rock slowly back and forth, my baby boy and me.
His little hand is feather light tucked up against my chin.
I hold his tiny hand in mine, and stroke his baby skin.
The house about us creaks and groans, the clock hands
creep around.
He snuggles closer to me still, and makes his baby sounds.
I love these quiet hours so much, and cherish every one.

All too soon he'll be grown up, his need for Mum gone.
But until then I still have time for kisses and for song.
Time for quiet hours like this with him cuddled in my arms.
Where I wish he'd always stay protected, safe and warm.
And yet I know the day will come when his tiny little hand,
will be bigger than my own. He'll grow to be a man.
But until then he's mine to love with no one here to see.
As we rock slowly back and forth, my baby boy and me.

Unknown

Geoffrey, Graham & Hazel, Cornwall 1990

Our children are carefree and I watch them with beady eyes as each milestone comes and goes. There is for me no greater joy than to be a part of this cycle of life. Never-ending and forever-changing from day to day, nothing more nothing less.

CHAPTER THIRTEEN

More About Father

Dad and the Motorbike and Tracie's Death

During my teenage years the lies my father told were quite unbelievable. He rode a motorbike and very occasionally would take mum out for a ride on it. On the front of one of his bikes was a fairing which was white, onto which he stuck an orange stripe saying he wanted people to think he was a police officer. He said it was great when people slowed down because they obviously thought he was. (*Pratt*) He had been spoken to on several occasions by the police and been told to remove it. He told us as children that he belonged to a special police force. When the telephone rang late in the evening he would say that it was the special police calling. The telephone would sometimes ring after midnight and off he would go, putting on his leathers and crash helmet, off into the night. I remember one evening in November 1976 he said he needed to go out because there had been a bundle that involved a gun, he was actually crying and I'd said to him he needed to chuck it in.

I didn't even think what other duties he might be performing. Only when I was much older it clicked that he was actually having an affair or performing other sinister activities. He would wait until the fat cow's (fc) husband went to work his night shift and off he'd go on his pretend missions for the special police. On occasions this fc and her husband would come to our house bringing sweets for the youngest children and for mum. Goodness knows what sob story my father was telling them, acting the dutiful husband and father in front of them. My mother never spoke; she just glared while my dad would usually have one of his daughters sitting on his knee. I learned recently that this wasn't the only lady he was having an affair with.

Then years later the (fc) passed away under very amusing circumstances, well to my warped sense of humour anyway. My father had been called out on an imaginary police job one evening and no guessing as to where he was. They say what goes around comes around and the (fc) went and died the next morning on his birthday. He was still at her house at this time – *well happy bloody birthday dad.*

Following her death we were now the lucky owners of her pet, a white, stinky poodle. The dog yapped all the time and was not my cup of tea at all. It didn't enjoy the best of health and it wasn't long before it had started to go to the toilet indoors. Dad would kick out at it, shouting abuse and yelling at it to shut up. He joked that he would give the fucking thing medication that belonged to my mother. Actually, that's just what he did and then buried the dead dog in the garden – no more yapping.

The poodle wasn't the only dog to live at 56. One day, when I was a teenager, quite out of the blue dad bought home a golden labrador retriever puppy. She was adorable and we named her Candy. I pretended she was just mine and I would take her out for long walks. Sometimes she would escape from the house and we would spend hours looking for her. As she grew she ate more and more until she eventually ate more than us. We would feed her Chappie dog food and I know for certain that some of my siblings ate the dog food when they were starving.

One day dad decided that Candy had to go; it was a

punishment for something I had done wrong. She didn't go straight away, I'd been out and when I arrived home she was gone. I cried for the loss of my close buddy. It later turned out that my father had ordered one of my brothers to take her to the chalk pits which would have taken my brother at least an hour to get to. The chalk pits were an isolated area of woods, pathways for walkers and disused pits. He was ordered to tie her up, leave her and come home, which of course he did for fear of being punished. We always did as we were told, for fear of what would happen if you disobeyed. A beating, his belt, a slipper or a thick ear. I went to the chalk pits in a state of total disbelief, tears in my eyes to look for her. I found the lead tied to a tree but no dog. I saw a few people and asked if they'd seen a loose dog. I was heartbroken. We also had kittens from time to time but they also went missing.

Dad's retirement

My father took early retirement at fifty to care for my mother; now that's a joke in itself. In my opinion he couldn't care for a blade of grass let alone take full responsibility for my mother. Thank goodness there were other siblings around to help. Father had always liked a drink of whisky and as time went by his addiction worsened. The bottles were hidden in different places around the house, all part of his denial. Because I had left home I wasn't always aware of the problems. He once said to me that he would be dead by the time he reached his sixtieth birthday. (*Hopefully I thought*)

Over the ten years that he was supposed to care for my mother I received numerous phone calls from my two youngest brothers. These calls were messages from my father passed on by my brothers, for my ears only. They were usually about what a terrible daughter I was. The words were obscene, unkind, cruel and untrue and I always said to my brothers its ok it's not your fault. Many times I would say to them, don't worry, just leave the swearing out he'll never know. As I placed the receiver down my heart would sink. After each and every call I would be upset, angry and sad for the two boys who had been ordered to deliver the messages to me from the local pay phone.

On one occasion I received a distressing call from a family member asking me to go over to the house to help. It was a desperate cry for help and it pulled at every string in my heart, how could I, not go! Without a thought I made my way over. My siblings were clearly upset and at a total loss as to what to do. Here I was, a mother to my own children and still acting the role of a mother to my siblings.

I was furious and by the time I'd got to the house I'd worked myself up into a terrible state. I went through the front door and straight up to my parents' bedroom. Sure enough they were both in bed and as I opened the door the stench hit me – cigarettes, whisky and stale body odour. I prodded my father and shouted at him to get up.

I said, 'You're meant to be looking after mum'.

I threatened him, saying if he didn't stop drinking, get up and clean mum up I'd contact the social services. I said I'd be back in a few days and stormed out. I felt awful leaving the others there but I had my own family to take care of now. For a while, on the surface anyway, things seemed to be normal – hum but what's normal?

I went with my father to appointments at the hospital when his drinking was particularly bad and during one of these appointments the consultant asked him to hold his hands out, palms facing up. He then asked me to do the same. My father's palms were a red colour mine were pink.

I listened to the consultant saying, 'Can you see the difference?'

'Yes,' my father said.

The consultant then went on to say, 'If you don't stop drinking, you won't be here in eighteen months'.

When the liver eventually became so damaged by alcohol his stomach became swollen with fluid and my father would go into hospital to have it drained off. He looked like he was about nine months pregnant. It was such an awful time. He started adding ice cream to cream soda and drinking that.

It was at this time that I made the decision to contact social services; my main concerns were that my mother wasn't being cared for. We had a fantastic social worker called Pam and she arranged a series of meetings. The first meeting took place on Thursday, November 1st 1990. Not all of my siblings were there but a vast majority were and a copy of the letter was sent to my father. This meeting was difficult to say the least.

* * * * *

The following letter was sent to my father from Pam Harvey.

Dear Mr Arm,

I am writing to you at the request of all your sons and daughters who came to the meeting on Thursday 1st November. (Kevin and Mandy did not come.) A number of issues, past and present were raised and talked about. Your children wanted you to know that:

• They don't want their mother to be taken out of the home if she can be looked after properly there. They want to help you and your wife.

• The appreciate the great step you have made in acknowledging that you have a drink problem and that you are accepting help with it, they would like you to continue to tackle the problem.

• They acknowledge that life was tough for them as children but they appreciate what you did to hold the family together and that you stuck to this whilst they were growing up.

• They want you to know that they have feelings and respect for you which they are unable to express and which they think you may not believe.

• They think that the way forward is by talking a lot, including in meetings such as this one with everyone present.

Your children had ideas about some practical ways in which we might be useful to you and we agreed to follow these up. One was to pursue the possibility of some day care for your wife, the other was to talk to you about what interests you might like to develop outside the home if we could find someone to care for Doreen at home. Your children also wanted to know more about the nature of their mothers illness and we agreed to ask a doctor to write something which we could give them at the next meeting.

Before the meeting ended, the team summarised their thoughts and gave your children a message. They wanted that message included in this letter so that you could hear it.

'We appreciate the effort you have all made to be here and all the rearranging of work and family commitments this involved. We are aware that there are very strong feelings around about the past for some of you which affect the present. Some of you are too frightened to go home to see your mother. Many of you would like to go home to see her and take her out to give her something more in life. Maybe you will find a way of doing this in groups.

We have been made very aware of your father's power in the family and we have felt his power in this meeting although he has been absent. Now you are all older and talking together, you also have power. Maybe your father knows this and fears this.

In order to help your mother, we feel that today's meeting may be the first step in helping your father to accept help for your mother.'

I am sending a copy of this letter to all your children.

We have arranged to meet again on Thursday 6th December between 3.30 and 5.00 p.m. You, your wife and all your children are invited to come.

Yours sincerely,
Pam Harvey
Social Worker

When my father passed away on April the 11th 1992, it was a glorious sunny morning. I'd been at the hospital all night with two of my sisters. We slept together in a small waiting room, our legs up on a small table and a blanket covering us. The nurses had been very kind and we took turns to go into the side room to see if he was still with us. I got up suddenly because I'd felt a whoosh come through the room and as I entered his room it was obvious to me he had died. The room stank, his head was turned to the left and his mouth was wide open. On the pillow was this horrid black stuff, which I later found out was tar from all the smoking. He was curled up in the foetal position. I remember I didn't feel sad, I just thought 'bloody good' and left the room to tell my sisters. We telephoned relevant family members then we left the hospital. One sister cried and I comforted her. The sun was shining and it was a glorious spring morning. People were going about their normal day to day stuff and my dad was dead in the hospital. I wanted to stop people and say, 'My dad just died'. I didn't of course; life goes on as normal.

I did cry at his funeral, but more from the feeling that at last I would be free of him. Seeing so many family members upset and for all the wrong reasons upset me more than his passing.

The funeral had been arranged by my older brother and I as we were the legal guardians and trustees. The service was held at the same church that I was christened and married in, St Mary's, Digswell. The burial followed at Hatfield Cemetery. I had looked at my mother on that day and we had exchanged silent glances that spoke a thousand words – I felt we were as one.

I had felt sick all day and kept thinking ok the bastard has died and that's that. Mum won't have to suffer at his hands any more; no more raping, no more violence, no more cruelty, no more filthy words. Some accounts from other family members are very different to mine. I'd heard he had mellowed with age and that they were cared for and fed; well that's good. In reality he was probably so far gone he didn't know what he was doing.

Special times with mum at Libury Hall care home

There were other things that needed to be sorted out now, mum for one. We needed to find a suitable place for mum to be cared for. Some family members I believe wanted to care for her and keep her in the family home. This could have been possible but it wasn't going to happen. We had a very good social worker at the time and my brother and I viewed a couple of residential homes that we thought would be suitable. In the end we chose a place in Great Munden called Libury Hall. There were spacious grounds with gardens and she could have her own room eventually. She was able to take her own bedroom furniture which I believed was a good idea so that she could have familiar things around her.

There were two brothers still living in the house and this also would need to be sorted out. There was no way the council would allow two young men to live in a four bedroomed council property. They were eighteen years old and twenty-one, but despite their ages, still very young and immature. I was sad for them as they were going to leave behind the only home they knew. They eventually moved into a flat together.

CHAPTER FOURTEEN

Finding Out About The Adopted Twins

When I was about fifteen years old I decided to have a snoop around in my parent's bedroom. Their bedroom was at the front of the house and nothing particularly special as far as I can remember. Mum had a large, dark, wooden dressing table with a big central mirror. On the dressing table she had a cream dressing table set with pink flowers painted on it, which included a brush, a mirror and a comb. She also had a few pieces of costume jewellery, a green stoned necklace and several brooches.

There was also one double and one single wardrobe in the room, both of which had keys in the locks but the doors had been left unlocked. I started looking through the pockets of father's clothes not really sure what I was hoping to find. In the back of my mind I probably wanted to find money or proof that he had been having an affair, something I had suspected for a long time. On the top shelf was an old square Oxo tin with a tightly-fitting lid. I remember feeling nervous about taking the lid off and about making too much noise, just in case someone should hear me. Looking through the different papers in the tin, I found their wedding certificate, the rent book and mum's Provident book from the Co-op. At the bottom of the tin underneath all the papers, folded neatly I found some papers that I did not recognise. They were titled

'Notice to Respondent of Application for Adoption Order'. My heart skipped a beat. I read through them as quickly as I could for fear of getting caught. The majority of it I did not understand, but there were two pages for mum and two for dad showing our old address at Knightsfield, Welwyn Garden City, Hertfordshire. I understood that they were an application for a boy named Peter and a girl named Christine (twins) to be adopted; a guardian had been appointed in Watford where the twins would go first. I started to feel excited to think that I may have another brother and sister somewhere. The date on the letter was 16th January 1962. By this time my sister Diane had come into the room and I told her exactly what I'd discovered.

It was during this period that I worked in Bartons the Bakers in the town centre on Saturdays. My auntie Lily, who was mum's sister, was the manageress there and I loved it, it made me feel important. I had a cream cake every week. Myself and some of the other girls use to hide one under the counter and eat it when there were no customers. Aunty Lily always gave me some of the stale bread and cakes to take home at the end of the day. The bread and cakes were always a treat for my younger siblings and mum of course.

I asked my auntie outright about the twins and her reply was, 'When you are older, I shall tell you all about it'.

'Crap!' I thought, I have already worked it out.

I remember also asking mum who Christine and Peter were. She must have been fairly coherent at this time, but her reply was also short, saying that 'two babies were left at the hospital'.

It all started to make sense. I had to pick my moment when to approach my father to ask about the twins. An opportunity arose during one of his many drinking sessions; I felt it was a good time because he seemed in a happy mood. I told him that I had found the papers but wasn't sure what they meant – I played a little dumb. He said it was Diane and Kevin and that he and mum had adopted them. It didn't take me long to work out that was a load of rubbish because the birth dates were different so there was no way the twins were Diane and Kevin.

The years passed by and I thought about the twins on many occasions, wondering who they might look like and where they were living. Sometimes I would see people and think they looked like members of my family. I always knew one day that they would either turn up on my doorstep or I would trace them.

Finding my Sister Sue

If it wasn't for an amazing organisation called NORCAP, my sister and I may never have met, though I'm sure we would have done eventually. I decided to try and trace the twins so I contacted the Salvation Army who were extremely helpful and gave me the address of NORCAP. I telephoned initially and they asked me to write a letter and I enclosed copies of birth certificates for the two babies. I thank my sister Mandy for getting these for me. I was contacted about a week later by letter and the information it contained knocked me for six. They believed a sibling had just registered and was also trying to trace their family. Now, how spooky is that I thought; registering at exactly the same time as me. There were no other details included in the letter, just a phone number requesting that I contact the organisation by phone, which of course I did.

Sue and Denise
The day we met Summer 1990

I was so nervous and excited, both my parents were still alive and I must admit it felt a little odd. I now had this secret. The lady I spoke to was very professional and asked details about my family and parents. She said she believed a birth sister was on the register but was not quite ready to continue. I understood fully and was happy to wait. At last I thought I've found you both.

My sister Sue telephoned on Monday, 16th July 1990 whilst I was babysitting for another sister who just happened to live next door. My husband came round and looked like a ghost. He was in a dreadful state and said, 'You'd better sit down'.

'Why?' I asked.

He just stood there and I started to get frustrated, 'Just tell me, has someone died?' I asked.

'No,' he replied and went on to explain that my adopted sister had telephoned and would be calling back shortly. I was beside myself, that's fantastic I thought.

My sister telephoned later that evening, it was lovely to hear her voice. I listened intently to her and tried to build a picture of exactly what she looked like. She was well spoken and I tried to sound the same, though I'm positive I didn't. She was married and had a daughter who was just over one year old. We had a lot to talk about and thirty years of catching up to do. I took photos of my siblings at every opportunity over the following week and put together an album for her. I cycled to town with the film to be developed; I had just enough money to cover the cost. I collected the photos when they were ready and completed the album for Sue.

We had our first meeting the week after that first phone call, at Milton Keynes shopping centre outside John Lewis. In my diary I'd written that it would be a day to always remember and it certainly was. I saw her first in a blue tee-shirt, her hair was dark just like my mother's, and she had the most beautiful smile. Best of all she had boobs. We asked a passerby to take our photo just for the record. We talked … we talked … and shopped.

At first our conversations via the telephone were mainly about day to day stuff. I was fascinated to understand why she had chosen me from all the siblings. She knew there were siblings older than her but she had no idea that there were also another seven younger, that must have been a shock for her. I believe her search started with checking birth records with the same surname. It wouldn't have been too difficult. She worked out rough dates when we may have married and found marriage certificates, mine included.

I've put it down to fate we registered with NORCAP at the same time.

My husband and I had our first visit to her home in 1990. As we drove up their drive and under an archway we came into a courtyard with a stone fountain to greet us. The house and garden were stunning.

We sat in the garden with the sun shining and drank champagne. I felt like I was from a different world and that I didn't belong there. Her husband made us feel welcome but there was something very serious about the whole day. I tried to watch my p's and q's. Growing up on a council estate with virtually nothing meant I had been raised in a totally different world from my sister's. I felt no envy, I have never been an envious person, I just felt different.

After that visit my sister would send parcels to me. Tee-shirts from Next all neatly wrapped and gift vouchers from Marks and Spencer, all of which were received with great affection and I loved it. She was my fairy godmother and still is. She also sent gifts for our children and spoiled them on their birthdays. She has always been a very generous, kind person and has helped me out on a few occasions for which I am thankful. Our worlds are very different but friends we are and will always be.

We spoke every week on the telephone in the early days, sometimes four or five times just getting to know each other. We had holidays together and as our families and commitments grew so did the space between us.

I couldn't drive at this time which surprised my sister. They kindly offered to buy me a car if I passed my driving test. I hadn't thought of it before because everything I needed was within walking distance or I could take the bus or train. I was so excited at the prospect of driving and having my very own car that I booked my lessons. I passed first time in August 1994 and shortly after Sue's husband Graham delivered my car. It was a Mini 850 and bright blue. The previous owner had been a district nurse and I took great joy in telling everyone the fact. I thought I was so lucky and spoilt. I was now totally independent and the car gave me the freedom to travel wherever I wanted. My children loved it and we had many days of fun driving and exploring different places. On one trip to the hospital for a dental appointment, I had driven on the M11 in the pouring rain. My eldest son was in the front and the other two in the back. The rain came through the seals around the windows and up through the floor we all roared with laughter.

On a few occasions I met at Sue's house my brother Steve (her twin), but he had made it very clear that he did not want to be part of my family, in his eyes he had just one sister. I totally respected his wishes and I have not had any contact with him for many years.

CHAPTER FIFTEEN

Mum's Death (2000)

When my mother passed away, for me it was a relief. She had been transferred from Libury Hall care home to a nursing home in Stevenage because her health had deteriorated. She was frail and she looked so old for a lady in her early sixties. She would look at me with her blue eyes; she knew so much but said so little. I would always feel so sad whenever I visited her and I used to cry silent tears on the journey home. One of things I've always wanted was normal parents, is that such a selfish thing? The day before she died I visited her and spoke quietly to her saying it was time for her to go now. I told her I knew what dad had been doing all those years and that she mustn't worry about it. I said we would all be ok. I felt numb with relief when she died, what a bloody waste of a life.

I went to the chapel of rest to see her, not because I wanted to say goodbye but to see what she looked like. I was curious. As I entered the room where she was laid out there was a strange stillness and silence in the air. She was laid quite high up on an alter, about the height of my waist, which seemed strange to me at the time. She was dressed in a green outfit, one of her favourites and she seemed larger than I'd remembered. She must have been so full of embalming fluid; I'm surprised she didn't burst. I looked at her and thought she doesn't look like my mum! There was stitching visible at the bottom of her neck from the post mortem and I remember thinking at the time that they could have asked for a scarf to cover it. I felt detached and alone. If this is what it's all about I thought, you can bloody well keep it.

Helping to organise my mother's funeral was, to say the least, traumatic. I and a few members of the family did not want her buried in the same plot as my father. I couldn't for the life of me understand why she should be buried with the man that had systematically raped, mentally and physically abused her and some of her children for so many years. It made no sense. My late father had controlled our lives for so long and was still doing it from his grave. There was even conflict when the funeral arrangements were being made. I remember having chosen a beautiful piece of classical music, Pachelbel's *Canon*, which I believed would be a lasting tribute to her. However, some members of the family didn't even have the decency to listen to it, they actually laughed. After speaking with my brother I left the house. He was in a difficult situation and I understood that, but at that time I did not feel part of the family and still don't to this day. However, I did give a poem which was added to the order of service. As for the final arrangements for the burial, she was buried in the same plot as my father. *Well, at least she was on top of him!!*

I visit the cemetery often and always remove things left by other people for my father. By not acknowledging the past and choosing to leave gifts for him, they are, in my eyes, in very sad places.

Standing at the edge of the grave as the minister was performing the last rights, I was calm and collected and started to say out loud that it was all wrong and that everyone needs to know what he did. I looked at my father's sister and said, 'Do you know what my father did to her and some of his children?'

I was getting strange looks from quite a few people, especially his family, but I really didn't care. It was the right time for me to speak the truth that had been kept hidden away for so long. It was time for the hidden skeletons in our family's closet to be revealed. I wanted to let them all know what had taken place not only with my father, but also with my father's father when I was just a little girl. It felt good to speak out loud at last. I was not, however, prepared for what followed. I'd hope this would bring us all closer together as a family; in fact it did the complete opposite.

Back at my brother's house where the reception was held afterwards, it seemed strangely silent. Talking seemed to cease as I walked into the kitchen. I acknowledged a few people that I recognised, and then I walked into the living room. I could see my sister Diane sitting, she was looking at me rocking and shaking her head. I was aware she was speaking, but her voice seemed shallow and she was talking rather fast. She said, 'No, please don't say anything, don't tell, not now, not now!'

I remember thinking, 'I'm not going to keep quiet any more'. I could hear voices inside my head and I was arguing with myself. I sat down and said to my aunty, 'He abused us you know'.

My sister became hysterical but I thought, 'I don't care'. All I wanted to do was to get the truth out in the open. It wasn't that I didn't care about other peoples' feelings, but I knew in my heart that sometimes things just needed to be said. I'd had so many different things going around in my head. I was later accused of making the abuse story up and that hurt me more than anything; even the actual abuse that I suffered at the hands of my grandfather and father. I decided that this was the time when I needed to detach myself from my so-called family. I isolated myself for five years as I knew no other way of coping with the inner pain that I was suffering.

I spoke to the lady who lived next door to my parents and she said she knew things weren't right. She said she could hear us crying and mum too. I'm still to this day astounded that she chose to do nothing about it. When I asked her why she hadn't phoned social services she told me that years ago she had promised my mother she wouldn't report any goings-on in the house. My mother had asked her to keep quiet because she didn't want the children to be taken away. She told me that on several occasions she had fed some of my siblings with a straw through the letter box because no one was in to take care of them. Apparently my mother had gone walkabout, something she did often – children home alone!

Mum would often leave the house and go missing for hours on end. It was so frightening not knowing where she was and we were usually the ones who would be sent out to find her. We were told to, 'Go and find your mother and don't come back until you have'. We would be scouring the streets desperately searching for her. Dad would say, 'She's down the lagoon with her fancy man'. One day we had been looking for her for what seemed like hours and it had started to get dark, and in the end the police were called. She was eventually found in a car park in Welwyn Garden City town centre. She didn't have a clue where she was as she was so spaced out from the medication she was taking. I remember father claiming that she had been raped by other men on more than one occasion and that not all her children were his, but someone else's. I'd love to have been someone else's child not his and I often think about that now.

Dreamt of my mother. I was the age I am now. She was sitting in our living room and she looked well, her hair was dark and just below her shoulder. She was telling me about the theatre and three different doors and three different layers. It was lovely to see her.

To dream of a person who has died that we have known usually refers to strong emotions we have had about that person.

Number 3 in a dream. Your ideas for stability and success will materialise. Freedom, bravery, fun, enthusiasm, brilliance, listlessness, over-confidence, impatience, lackadaisical behaviour.

CHAPTER SIXTEEN

Charity Parachute Jump for Ali

Saturday, March 25th 2000
Alicia Jade Parks is my beautiful niece.

On Thursday, August 6th 1998 my sister Mandy telephoned with the most wonderful news, she was expecting a baby. We had waited and waited for such a long time for this day to come and I had to sit down because for me the news was overwhelming. We were thrilled to bits and I'd written in my diary that I couldn't quite believe it. There would be a brother or sister for Sam, at last.

The phone rang at 6.30 a.m. on March 28th 1999; Mandy was having contractions every ten minutes. 'I'm on my way,' I said and drove the 150 miles in less than two and a half hours. It didn't take long to realise we needed to get to the hospital as soon as possible, this baby was not hanging around.

I arrived at the hospital at ten twenty and Alicia was born at ten thirty five. Now that was close. This little baby girl weighed just 5lb 12oz. I knew at once that something wasn't quite right … I love you Mandy, that's what I'd written in my diary.

Nothing fitted this tiny little bundle…Mandy cried.

March 29th 1999
Sam and I went to bed early.
Took Sam for a walk, she told me she loved me and I her too.

April 2nd 1999
I went home feeling very sad.

I had decided to do something to raise some money for Alicia and opted to do a parachute jump. It was something I'd always fancied doing. I needed a letter from my doctor to say I was fit and well. When I was twenty-one years old Neil and I were looking at life insurance policies and both were asked to have full medicals. My doctor on close examination found I had a heart murmur. This was investigated and I was informed I had Mitral Valve Incompetence.

Mitral regurgitation is sometimes called mitral insufficiency or mitral incompetence. In mitral regurgitation the valve does not close properly. This causes blood to leak back (regurgitate) into the left atrium when the left ventricle contracts. Basically, the more open the valve remains, the more blood regurgitates. This increases the pressure in the left atrium and in the blood vessels coming from the lungs. This may lead to various problems and symptoms, depending on the severity of the leak. Medication can help to ease symptoms. Surgery to repair or replace the valve may be needed.

Thankfully to date I have not needed any treatment, though I do have high blood pressure which I take medication for daily and will continue to do so for the rest of my life.

The parachute jump took place on Saturday, March 25th 2000 two days after my mother passed away. I thought about not doing it but after much consideration decided I would; in my own words I was in shock from my mother dying so any nerves I had about the jump faded into nothing. I raised one thousand five hundred pounds and the company my husband

Good job done

Flying high from 10,000 feet

worked for matched it. I raised a grand total of three thousand, not bad for just jumping out of an astrapped to a hunky man. The actual jump took my breath away and the adrenalin rush started at my feet and travelled up the length of my body. It was amazing. I'm so glad I did it for Alicia.

If Alicia could speak this is what she would say:

The way the medical profession describe my condition is Congenital Cytomegalovirus (CMV) which has caused Microcephaly (small head), Spastic Quadriplegia (disordered control of movement), Visual Impairment and Development Delay.

Cytomegalovirus (the large cell virus) is a common virus and about 50 per cent of the population of Britain have been infected with it at some time.

If a woman catches CMV during her pregnancy the virus may sometimes be passed on to the foetus. If this happens some babies may be damaged. Only 10 per cent of affected babies will display symptoms and in only half of these children will the disability be serious; 90 per cent of affected children are perfectly healthy.

Unfortunately I was one of the babies with serious disabilities. My condition affects only 1 in 100,000 children. The virus has left me with severe brain damage and as a consequence I now have problems moving my limbs in a co-ordinated manner. I am unable to sit, crawl or do anything for myself. Although my eyes work well, my brain is unable to process the information they send, this condition is known as Cortical Blindness. In order to stimulate my senses my family is advised to spend as much time as possible playing with me using sound, light and touchy feely toys. Now at 13 years old my cerebral palsy has caused my spine to curve and I am currently on the waiting list for spinal surgery.

In order to try to increase my mobility a great deal of time is also spent providing physiotherapy and massage.

As you can imagine I require a lot of specialist equipment which is taking over my family's home. My parents have been fund-raising throughout my life and managed to build me my own special room. Today they are fund-raising for a new pushchair, so I can go on holiday and we are awaiting a new bathroom with a tracking hoist so I can save my mum and dad's backs, with an up and down bath.

Thank you Mandy for the above.

CHAPTER SEVENTEEN

Careers Are For Men, Not Women

I really wouldn't like say that I've had a career as such, but I have had many varied jobs along the way. My first job at nine years old (or probably younger) is a job no child should ever have to do. I became a carer to my mother and a mother figure to my younger siblings.

'Careers are for men, not women' … *echoes from the past.* Well that's what my father said and if he said it, it must be right and true.

At one time I did have thoughts and dreams of becoming a PE teacher or joining the army, that wasn't to be. It makes me sad to think of my lost opportunities, the lost years and what might have been or what I may have become. Then I am reminded of my life today, the journey, yes, my journey. I have had it said to me on many occasions; you wouldn't be the person you are today if you hadn't had those things happen to you. I would like to shout at those people …'Well thank you very bloody much', but I don't. I would like to have been given the choice, but sadly as babies and children we don't have a choice. Our parents, carers, adults, they are the ones who choose for us. Then the scars are so deep like a cancer, nibbling away at your very soul. When, if we are lucky, we find ourselves questioning our very existence, then and only then the painful journey can begin.

In my teens I worked in a bakers shop, did a milk round and delivered news papers. The in late in 1977 I had my first full time job working at the QE2 Hospital in Welwyn Garden City in the sterile products department. (See more about this job in the section 'Take a Chance On Me' on page 149).

I left the job at the hospital in early 1981 just prior to the birth of our first child. For the next fifteen years I took on the role of a full time mum. I was always busy, not just with my immediate family, as I made time to help at the local play group, teach at the Sunday school, run my own childminding business and do the odd morning at Oxfam.

Working at Oxfam was short-lived, mainly because the lady in charge had questioned me about an item that had been put on display that should not have been sold. I tried to explain that I did not have anything to do with it. She was clearly cross and bordering on bursting a blood vessel, as she hardly seemed to come up for air. She was right in my face and asked, 'Do you have any initiative?' To which I replied, 'Yes, and you can stick the job'. I promptly left the shop never to return.

All those jobs were very rewarding in there own right but I would just like to say that being at home with my three children has been the most rewarding job of all. To witness all of them take their first steps, be there on their first day at school and see the sheer delight on their faces as they come out the school gate, was priceless. I wouldn't have changed that for the world.

In 1994 I worked initially as a part time volunteer in a special needs school, which then led to full-time and part-time paid work. Working alongside David, Penny and Wendy were some of the most memorable and happy days of my working life. I left in April 2001 to start a job at Papworth Hospital in the surgical booking office and spent the next three years there.

Dear Diary

Friday, July 19th 2002
Today I decided to go to the doctors. I really must try and sort myself out once and for all. I spoke to the doctor about my childhood and how I have been feeling. I was very tearful; usually I kept my feelings under control and very rarely shed any tears. She prescribed anti-depressants, I wasn't really sure about that. (*Aren't they for mad people?*) She also referred me to a psychologist and a psychiatrist.

Saturday, July 20th 2002
The medication has made me sick, but Neil said it's just the side effects. I have spoken to Hazel, just so she knows and understands.

Monday, July 22nd 2002
I feel calmer.

Tuesday, July 24th 2002
I spoke to my boss, she was okay.

Day six, just a strange dazed feeling – tiredness and sickness has gone.

The appointment for me to see the psychologist and psychiatrist came and went. I arrived for my appointment at the health centre and as I entered the room where two guys greeted me. My tummy churned, I said to them both, "You can't help me, because you are men." I left. My doctor was not very pleased with me. I didn't care…

Sunday, September 14th 2003

I really need to lose some weight. What a shock in the mirror, you fat cow! Started to record everything I ate.

1 yogurt
Soup for lunch
1 pear, 1 apple, 1 orange

Bloody heck I've just got to shift this weight.

Monday, 15th September 2003

1 Wetabix
1 egg salad
1 apple, 1 pear, 1 banana.
Beans on toast.

Day 13 of the diet

Special K
Soup for lunch
1 banana, 2 pears, 1 yogurt

This way of eating continued for six weeks, needless to say the weight shifted.

I've always watched what I eat and feel tremendously guilty when I have an alcoholic drink or a snack. I am in control and will not become fat.

In July 2004 I decided I fancied a change and applied for a job at local Funeral Directors. I've always been inquisitive and I needed a new challenge; this one sounded right up my street. This did indeed turn out to be a challenging role and my life would take a completely different change in direction. During my time there, Neil and I would enter a phase of our marriage that can only be described as catastrophic and life-changing. I was going through a difficult time in my life and it is only now that I can look back and understand that not only was I menopausal but also in a very sad, lonely place. I would listen to the other guys at work laughing, joking and found myself joining in which made me feel like a completely different person. The guy in charge seemed to take a special interest in me and I was flattered. He would say nice things to me daily; touch my hair and best of all he always smiled. (*Or so I thought*) Needless to say I fell for him, hook, line and sinker. We talked together about family, life and shared our dreams and passions. I couldn't see any wrong in him and I couldn't wait to go to work or cover any extra shifts just so I could spend time with him. Sometimes he would behave in a way that I didn't like and alarm bells would ring, but I chose to ignore them. They say love is blind …

At home I was sad, depressed and looking at a husband who I felt was too busy to even notice me. In fact he was also in a very sad place and at a loss as to what to do. He started counselling and was taking antidepressants to try and help him cope. He was signed off from work and spent many days just sitting in our conservatory staring into space. This reminded me of my mother – *a powerful trigger I just didn't know it.* I was in my world and he was in his. The days, weeks and months passed by and Neil and I hardly spoke. We slept separately and I had sought advice from a solicitor about obtaining a divorce. This was no life for either of us, something had to change and as usual it had to be me that initiated it. I started the ball rolling by telling my husband that I didn't want to stay married and that I didn't love him anymore. Neil just sat in the chair and said nothing, nothing, nothing, and same old, same old. That was one of the most frustrating things about our relationship, he always said nothing, perhaps if he had fought back things would have been different. On that particular day, I felt I had indeed married my mother. The silences were driving me crazy and my anger was slowly rising.

I made my feelings very clear to the guy at work and he started to text me and left notes saying he loved me and missed me when we were apart. That was my green light, I was prepared to leave Neil and build a new life for myself. Whatever hurdles were put in my way I knew I would gladly face because I was in love and it felt like it was the first time in my life.

Then something changed...

A new lady came to work in the office. I had been away on annual leave and as I went through the office door I noticed the desks had been turned around to face each other. She was sitting in my desk and he was playing with her hair! I felt sick. I had no where to sit. This man who I believed had loved me, started to make fun of me and teased me, saying I would need to learn the accounting side of the job. I hated anything to do with figures and he knew it. For a brief moment I saw him as my father, a Jekyll and Hyde character and from that moment I made my mind up to leave. Whatever happened I knew I would cope, even if that meant that I would be alone.

When I returned home after work I didn't know what to think or what to do. I had lost so much weight I was beginning to look anorexic. I wasn't eating or sleeping properly and contemplated suicide – what else could I do? I spent some time staying with my sister Sharon and tried to sort my head out. It was a relief to talk to her, although at this point I had never really discussed my abuse with her. In my eyes she had always loved her father and seen no wrong in him. That was her world not mine.

Eventually I returned home and Neil was furious. For the first time I was frightened of him because he looked at me with so much hatred in his eyes. He told me I had used him as a meal ticket …

How strange that you can live with a person for so many years, love them and care for them and then slowly over time begin to dislike everything about them. The way they sit, how they eat and even breathe. I grew to dislike Neil with such hate that I wished him dead and out of my life forever. I imagined he had been killed in an accident while out driving, in fact I played out many different scenarios in my head all with different endings. I imagined being with a great hunky rugby player who towered above me and protected me. Not Neil with his tall, thin body.

I spent nearly two years sleeping on the floor in our bedroom or in a separate room. I didn't want him anywhere near me. He would say to me , 'Why do you always push me away, always putting up a barrier?' I love to be held tightly, but hate the feeling of being let go. In my head I felt it was easier to not be held, then I didn't have to experienced being let go. It's a funny thing but I've never felt safe in Neil's arms… I probably wouldn't feel safe in any man's arms … ***damaged goods that's what I am.***

This is when I felt most vulnerable because I knew I didn't have a well paid job and would not be able to support myself. I felt trapped and the doubt started to creep in. 'What do you think your are doing Denise? You are so ungrateful, your husband has provided for you and this is how you repay him.'

We had a short spell of relate counselling but it was hard for me to listen and hear what Neil had to say about me. The counsellor asked him if he had ever considered leaving me and the silence that fell into the room spoke a thousand words. A lot is communicated through silence. My tummy churned deep inside and I felt like a little girl lost. We looked at each other with sadness. I had always put Neil on a pedestal but that day it had been taken away. Here I was feeling lost and alone, the same … always the same … on my own. Neil asked me, 'Why don't you trust me'?

Unfortunately I can't answer that question because I don't trust anyone. When you trust people they always let you down, so by not trusting I knew I wouldn't be let down again. This is something he had thrown in my face often and I hated him for it because I couldn't explain why I didn't trust him, I just didn't. I reminded him of a party that we had been to years ago. When we returned home and made our way up to our bedroom we kissed and hugged. He whispered into my ear, 'Lift your skirt up *****'; he had called me by another female name. I replied, 'I'm wearing trousers and that's not my fucking name'. Today, in 2012, I am still sickened by the very thought that he called me by another name. Is this what men do? Fantasise about other women and call out their names. He says he doesn't remember, but I will always remember even though for the present I push the thought to the very back of the closet.

We decided as a last resort to go away for a week and spend some time together getting to know one another again. I felt I had nothing to lose and was not ashamed of the way I had felt towards the other guy. I felt I had always been totally honest. We both spoke openly, honestly and truthfully, probably for the first time in our marriage. We learnt new things about each other and cried until we were totally exhausted. We had turned a corner and we held each other with new found love, but no sex.

CHAPTER EIGHTEEN

Grenada and My Empty Nest Syndrome

Late in 2007 I was feeling increasingly restless and had a general feeling of loneliness. An older female colleague at work commented that I may have something called 'empty nest syndrome'. Great, thanks for that, I thought to myself. I'd heard and read about different women doing crazy and not so crazy things at this changing and challenging time of their lives. So I decided I needed to do something for that just involved me. I felt like two different people, at work I would pretend that everything was fine, but inside I was totally lost.

I had just started a period of specialist counselling in Cambridge and for the first time in my life I felt I was being heard. My nights were filled with dreams that I didn't understand, days of reoccurring flashbacks and this is when I began recording them in a journal. I wrote everything down even if it didn't appear to make any sense. I felt my choices were limited at the time because money was tight. I did, however, have a bonus that was due at the end of March 2008 and I decided that it would be perfect to cover the costs of whatever life-changing decision I made.

Some younger members of the team at work had been talking about voluntary gap years and I'd listened with interest. I felt quite envious of them being able to just take off for a year. I was fascinated with the choices and options that were available to them and this in turn inspired me into thinking about voluntary work. After my early 6 a.m. shift of baking finished, I couldn't wait to get home to begin my search. I'd already made my mind up unconsciously that I'd be going away, I just didn't know where or when. I arrived home and the house was empty, my 'empty nest' – my three fledglings had flown. I turned the radio on for background noise, made myself a cup of tea, took a soya yogurt from the fridge and sat down at the computer.

As my search began on line I was completely bowled over by the numerous choices and different types of voluntary work available and not just in the United Kingdom. I typed volunteers abroad and pressed the enter button. One site caught my eye and the choice of voluntary work they offered covered one hundred and fifty countries worldwide. I decided to explore further. The list was vast with options from a Tibetan teaching programme to a conservation programme watching wild wolves in Iceland. It didn't take me long to make up my mind. There were a few age stipulations which ruled out some of the programmes but I didn't allow this didn't deter me. The Ocean Spirits leatherback turtle programme in Grenada kept jumping out from the page. I answered their questions with ease – I can walk on soft sand for two–three miles in the heat, have a great sense of humour and am looking for a new challenge.

That's the easy bit. As a research assistant on the programme my duties would include:

Night patrols of the main leatherback nesting site
Flipper tagging of unmarked females
Data collection – carapace (shell) measurements, egg counts, nest relocation

Morning surveys (on foot)
Nest excavations
Maintenance and preparation of research equipment
Assisting with organised turtle watches for schools
Camp maintenance and cleaning

Ocean Spirits is a registered, non-profit marine conservation organisation based in Grenada trying to prevent the extinction of marine turtles found throughout the country's coastal waters and beaches. Grenada is known as the Spice Isle because of its high production of nutmeg and is also one of the least spoilt of the Caribbean islands. Levera beach is a major nesting site for the leatherback turtle and most of the research takes place there. I applied on line and was accepted onto the programme. I was elated when I received the news and couldn't wait to tell my closest family and anyone else who may be interested.

I just couldn't take it in that I would actually be going to Grenada the following April. The time soon came around, however, and as April approached I was packed and ready to go. The list of essential items was endless from mosquito nets to insect spray, infra-red light, medication to stop my periods, my new iPod with all my favourite tunes – thank you Geoffrey – a sleeping bag and of course, not forgetting my diary and a brand new blank journal to record my adventures. So my packing was complete.

Sleep didn't come easy the night before I left. I tossed and turned until the alarm clock 'wake up gromit, time for walkies' went off at 3.30 a.m. – I hate that bloody alarm clock. I felt nervous and rushed about like a headless chicken as I prepared to leave. Neil kindly got up with me and drove me to Gatwick

Airport. There was hardly any traffic and the journey was perfect. I was cold, nervous and excited when we arrived, all rolled into one. We found a café and I had a hot chocolate while Neil had coffee, passing the time with ideal chit chat. Neil had no idea that I had pre-ordered a dozen red roses to arrive two days later in celebration of our twenty-eighth wedding anniversary. I smiled inwardly. We had never been apart on our anniversary; he had given me a card which was tucked safely in my hand luggage.

When it was time to go to the departure lounge, Neil held my hand tightly and we walked together. We said our goodbyes and hugged each other. Neil cried as I left to go through the gates and I called back to him, 'I'm coming back, you know'. Emotion is something I rarely do.

It's 8.20 a.m and I'm sitting on my own in the departure lounge. Now Neil has gone it's a very strange feeling being completely on my own. Looking at the busyness of the airport and the comings and goings of all the different people I feel detached. I decided to go and choose a book, but ended up purchasing a lipstick instead, goodness knows why.

I boarded the plane at 8.40 a.m. and waited for half an hour before take-off. I sat next to a guy who was travelling to Trinidad to visit his sick mother. We had polite conversations on and off during the nine-hour flight. For most of the flight I felt nauseous and had a headache as it dawned on me, 'I'm really going – too late to turn back now'. I told myself firmly that I was a middle-aged woman embarking on a journey of self-discovery. I fantasised about meeting a stranger and having wild sex in all kinds of places – well I'm only human.

Probably not a good idea anyway, I don't want to catch some horrible germs. The plane started its decent.

Leaving the aircraft, the air felt warm on my skin and I took a deep breath to prepare myself for what was ahead of me. The sky was clear and the sun shone like a friendly face and I knew I'd be ok; in fact I've always known I'd be ok.

A taxi driver was waiting for me with my name on a board which he held in the air so that I wouldn't miss him. I was a little unsure of getting into the taxi with a strapping, rather scruffy, coloured man but he gave me a very large grin showing off his perfect white teeth. I'm definitely not having sex with him (*joke*). The rhythmic Caribbean music blared from the radio and the journey took no more than ten minuets. The houses were mostly wooden and looked as though they needed a good coat of paint. The driver drove at speed and turned off down a dusty, well-worn track. I hung onto my seat imagining that he was about to mug me! We arrived shortly afterwards at the True Blue hotel where I would stay for one night. I was very pleasantly surprised.

I had help from the receptionist to get my case up the stairs; I'd never have managed it on my own. Looking back now I'd taken far too much stuff, especially shoes. Once in the room I collapsed onto the bed for a brief moment. I found some energy from goodness knows where to locate the rich tea biscuits and headache pills from inside my case. My ankles had swollen quite badly and my head was thumping leaving me feeling quite woozy. For the next two hours I just lay like a corpse on top of the bed covers, surrounded by beautiful, delicately-perfumed flower petals that had been sprinkled onto the bed.

When I thought my headache had subsided enough for me

to move, I gingerly made my way to the bathroom. That felt ok so I decided to peep outside. I felt like spy, but to my delight I discovered I had my own private balcony with a plastic white sun lounger. The sun was shining and the view was breathtaking, with beautiful blue skies and crystal clear water stretching for miles. Looking out across the sea I suddenly realised I felt lonely and I thought of my husband Neil and how he would have loved it. I missed him terribly. As I sat down on the lounger and started to close my eyes, a movement in a tree in front of me made me jump, it was a small black bird. Welcome back to reality I thought.

I returned to my room and thought how lovely it was and how lucky I was to be having this whole new experience. The room was filled with bright colours everywhere from the curtains down to the bedding. The room had everything I needed. I was going to order some food but changed my mind. It was already 17.50 and I was ready for bed – I slept soundly for the next ten hours.

It had rained during the night and I woke at 4.00 a.m. and listened to the dawn chorus. I sent my daughter Hazel a text message to wish her luck for her job interview. I could hear the birds outside and although I was not sure what they were, they were incredibly noisy. At 8.00 a.m. I ordered via the telephone in my room, a light breakfast of fruit, toast, juice and tea. That should see me through until lunch, I thought and then later if I'm still hungry I may try the flying fish sandwich (*I hope its dead*)!

A cleaner arrived at 15.30 and talked about hurricane Ivan and the devastation it had caused her family in September 2004. I gave her a tip of about $20 which was probably far too much – oh well.

I had nothing to eat for lunch as my body clock was all over the place. Later when I started to feel a little peckish I ordered a shrimp curry, which was delicious. That cost me seventy-five Caribbean dollars. I showered, applied sun tan oil, changed into a vest and shorts and then ventured outside to explore. To my delight the place was brimming with wildlife. I nearly fell over a mongoose and there were so many species of lizard I didn't know where to look first. The birds were abundant from the tiniest humming bird to birds I didn't recognise at all.

It was beautiful, calm and serene. I smelt spices in the warm air and the sweet scent of flowers. The True Blue hotel accommodation was a mixture of small apartments and villas, all of which had spectacular views of the sea. I walked along a raised wooden pier, and peering over the edge I could see tiny crabs running back and forth over the muddy surface where the sea had receded. I strolled around the small complex greeting the few people that I passed. I found the swimming pool and took a dip; oh what bliss. Only when I'd made my way back to my room did I notice I'd burnt across my shoulders from the hot midday sun.

My journey continued the following day. The taxi arrived at 12.30 with a driver and another female volunteer. We were told the journey to our accommodation would take approximately an hour and a half. The roads were, to say the least, interesting. There was lots of hooting, honking and the driver shouting 'How's tings?' (*how are things*) out of the taxi window. Once again the music blared. The whole experienced was great and I was starting to feel really good about my decision.

The accommodation was situated at the north-east of the island, a windswept piece of paradise with incredible views across the outer islands and Carriacou. The inside of the accommodation left a lot to be desired, though. I have never stayed in such a dirty, disgusting place in my whole life and my heart sank. I'm not sure if the look of horror was evident on my face to the other volunteers, if not I must have hidden it well. Actually I was very good at hiding my true feelings. The first thing I did was make my bed with clean sheets, put up my mosquito net and gave it a good spray down with repellent. I don't think the room had been cleaned for months. The two windows were behind bright red metal bars; in fact the whole house was encased in red metal bars; a little worrying I thought.

The other housemates included three females and four guys all of whom seemed fairly normal, thank goodness. The following day was spent getting to know each other and learning about the work we would be doing. I was the oldest member of the team and was referred to as 'mum'.

The gardens surrounding the house were wild and free. The fauna was beautiful and there was wildlife to be seen in every direction, particularly the large lizards and brightly-coloured humming-birds.

My first night duty wouldn't be until Tuesday and I looked forward to it. I'd been bitten the evening before by mosquitoes and other biting insects most probably bed bugs, and the red swollen bites were driving me crazy. A trip to the beach where the night work was to be carried out was a welcoming break. I was, however, saddened by the rubbish that had collected on the beach. I had imagined a long, unspoilt, yellow, sandy beach, not one strewn with old metal drinks cans, plastic bags and general everyday rubbish. The day ended with a video of the turtles and a brief overview of the next month. I was tucked up in bed by nine o'clock under a white mosquito net and sprayed from head to foot in repellent. I had my earphones in and drifted off to sleep to the sound of Michael Jackson singing. Tomorrow would be an early start at five fifteen.

The alarm sounded from my phone and I made my way to the bathroom. I was greeted by the cockroaches and bid them good morning. Actually I was thinking to myself 'horrible bloody things' but I knew I would just have to get used to them hiding in the cupboards and every nook and cranny.

This was my first early survey on Bathway beach and I found walking on the soft sand hard going but was determined not to give up. If anything, I thought, this will do my legs the world of good. There was evidence of new turtle nests but also of poachers. Bathway beach is not a place that is patrolled in the evening so there was plenty of opportunity for poachers to take advantage of the eggs and turtles. However, there was talk that the patrols were going to be increased but at present the project only has enough staff to patrol in the mornings, not in the evenings.

That evening was to be my first night duty and I hoped I would see my first Leatherback turtle. I was so excited as we prepared to leave. I was dressed from head to toe in dark clothing and although my rucksack felt heavy on my back, I didn't care. With my sleeping bag tucked under my arm, an infra-red light on my forehead and numerous pieces of equipment for the research that we would be carrying out, I definitely looked the part, not quite sure if I felt it though.

We left at seven p.m. and it was pitch black, just as well the guys know the way I remember thinking. Two Grenadian guys

Cliff and Praggie were joining us for the night shift and we collected them en route to the beach. The Grenadian guys that joined the group every evening would eventually take over the running of the project. Levera beach was deserted. Once we had parked up and unloaded, we made our way to the far end of the beach. Most evenings we would turn an old fishing boat on its side to use as a base and for shelter if the wind changed direction. The sea crashed onto the shore, there was very little light and it took me a while to adjust.

We hadn't been on the beach long and Geoff, who was one of the supervisors, whispered to me to keep very still and lie down as a turtle was emerging out from the sea. I could see a faint shadow which looked like a rock in the water. Slowly, this magnificent prehistoric-looking creature made her way up out of the water onto the sand. I was mesmerised. The sheer size of her took my breath away. With every breath in and out she sounded as if it would be her last and I quite forgot what I was there for. I watched her choose a nest site, dig a chamber and prepare it before finally depositing her eggs. I was privileged to lay with her and count the rubbery eggs as each one fell into my hands. I placed with care the small golfball-sized, white eggs into the chamber one by one. I felt her every contraction as a new batch of eggs descended into my palms. Once this part of the cycle was completed the female turtle covered the eggs with sand. During the egg-laying session the turtle's shell is measured and she is tagged and microchipped. A record is also made of the nesting site. The following morning, in daylight, the information is logged and turtle tracks raked so that the poachers cannot find the nests. We had over fifteen turtles that night and after the nightshift ended at seven thirty a.m. I was

Leatherback turtle making her way back to sea
'a good job done'

The most amazing sight

exhausted, but happy, as we drove back to camp. This pattern was repeated many times over the next four weeks.

During some of the night surveys we would be joined by vet/medical students from St Georges University. I felt some of them were a pain in the backside. The students were very noisy and took photographs with the flash on when we had specifically asked them not to. On other occasions tourist groups would come to observe and take photographs. I was grumpy on one occasion because I'd been bitten by a centipede and I made sure everyone knew it. I repeatedly asked a student not to take photos and he was clearly not happy with me.

Geoff, myself and Emily at the rum factory and, yes, the bottle is just about empty.

Happy Days and Rum

A visit to the seventeenth-century rum factory was all it was cracked up to be. Health and safety eat your heart out; it simply doesn't exist here. We had the most amazing tour and drank a bottle of seventy-two percent rum between the four of us. We needed the walk home to sober up – oh boy the rum punch was very good.

Tuesday, 22nd April and I was missing my home comforts after having been bitten again. I have counted nearly two hundred bites and most of them are on my bum, I am a little fed up to say the least. Tomorrow is my eldest son's birthday and this is the first time I've not seen him on his birthday in twenty odd years.

Local school children after a clean up at Bathway beach

During my time in Grenada we visited a local school. The children were a delight, laughing and calling us the 'white people'. This part of the programme was to educate the children about the turtles and the value they bring to Grenada. The children were fascinated by the dead hatchling in a jar and the eggs, but I was surprised by their lack of knowledge and understanding of such a critically endangered species, living in their country. All the while someone is planning to build a hotel and golf complex on Levara beach.
Then I received a message from my daughter to say she had been offered the job at the hospital – phew what a relief.

Days Off and Sightseeing

Myself, and two other female volunteers, had decided to take the bus to Grenville. Just the three-fifty dollar bus ride was worth it as I've never seen so many people crammed onto a bus. Just when I thought you couldn't get any more people on, another seat was found and three more spaces were created. We passed wooden houses of all shapes, sizes and colours and outside most of these houses were small wooden constructions which held fruit and vegetables for sale. There was singing, laughing and just general banter on the bus. The driver seemed to shout out from the bus at random passerbys, but I soon worked out that that is just what they do. It's their way of saying hi! There didn't appear to be any bus stops, people simply held out their hand and the bus stopped. We visited the fish market which was enormous and stank to high heaven. I had never seen so many different varieties of fish. On a separate visit Emily and I also travelled to the capital of St Georges. Once again we were on the bus, not a seatbelt

Counting turtle eggs

The tracks of time

to be seen and packed in like a tin of sardines. The roads were windy and treacherous in places and we had to hang on to prevent ourselves from being tossed about. We decided to buy a few gifts to take back home and spices seemed the obvious choice. The smells were divine and the ladies selling the gifts were colourful, loud and above all friendly. It was a joy to me to listen to their stories. They gave us some free vanilla liquid which turned out to be a favourite back home.

After Emily and I had drunk a banana and cherry smoothie we sat down on a low wall which looked out over the harbour. We witnessed some guys dragging a turtle upside down with a rope around its neck. They pulled it onto a trolley and made their way towards the fish market. The turtle was alive and clearly in distress. This episode made me realise the importance of our work here, but it was also a stark reminder that I was in a foreign country and this was normal behaviour for them. I put my video away quickly as I didn't want anyone to see that I had filmed what had just taken place. Emily and I then made our way back to the bus stop. I showed the others in the team the video when I returned; they were sickened but not surprised. It is illegal to fish turtles here.

Later in the afternoon Emily and I walked to the beach from our accommodation. We walked along the sand and swam in the sea at Bathway, the whole experience was blissful and carefree. The locals had said the salty water would be good for my bites, I had certainly hoped so as they were driving me crazy. A small shop selling local goods, mainly for tourists, was situated near the beach so we browsed and I bought a shell necklace and a small keyring golly. I have enjoyed Emily's company immensely; she is like a breath of fresh air. We ended our trip to the beach by eating chips and drinking lager. I knew the guys at home would laugh when they heard what I'd been up to. 'Me, drinking lager, surely not.' The day ended with catching up on some hand washing, a chore I did most days, and luckily in the warm air it never took long to dry.

The day before I was due to leave, myself and the other three female volunteers took the bus to Saulters for a final lunch out. We ate, drank and toasted each other to love, life and happiness.The girls stopped off on the way back at the pool bar and I made my way back to base to finish my packing. I felt a little out of sorts and rather sad. The experiences and memories I have of that unique place will stay with me forever. The people of that island were some of the most beautiful, kind and genuine I have ever had the pleasure of spending time with and I shall miss them.

Back at The True Blue Hotel

My last day in Grenada and I treated myself to a full cooked breakfast. My sister Sue would have been proud of me. Salt fish, coconut bakes, fried plantain, egg, fresh local juice, sliced seasonal fruit and, of course, tea, all for the princely sum of EC $30.00.

As this unique experience came to a close I looked back and reflected on my time there with some sadness. I've learned things about myself that I wasn't consciously unaware of, in particular the fact that I found it so difficult to let myself go and truly relax. One of the reasons for choosing to go to Grenada was to try and discover and work out who I really was. Looking back on my experience I came to the conclusion that, yes, I could travel anywhere in the world but, wherever I go I am still the same person with the same feelings whether away or at home. I often reflect on my counselling and how far I have advanced, but somehow I still feel something is missing. I do not feel a complete person and that I believe is my lost childhood and the loss of my mother's love.

I have met some truly remarkable people with their own stories to tell, some of which are tragic. I have also discovered a little piece of me that I didn't know existed before I came to this wonderful island. For the first time in my life I'm finding out about me and starting to accept myself for who I truly am. I have had times during this vacation when I have felt totally at peace and other times when I just felt I didn't fit in. All the other people during my time here have accepted me unconditionally, even before they knew a little of my past. I now know I am a survivor and am facing the unknown years ahead with my head held high and dealing with the pain involved in my own unique journey.

CHAPTER NINETEEN

What Happened in Jersey?

During the time of my counselling in Cambridge, I was reading through my old diaries and came across some notes I'd made. I had written that my father had gone to Jersey on November 18th 1978. I have no idea why he went but I knew he had gone with a male friend, or so he had told us. Watching the news in the summer of 2007 I couldn't help but notice the coverage in the news regarding the Haut de la Garenne children's home on the island of Jersey. The case involved former residents of the home claiming they had been beaten, sexually abused and had soap forced into their mouths by those responsible for their care.

I went cold just thinking about it – surely my father was not involved in something as sinister as that. I put it to the back of my mine for a while. Because I'd kept a diary I decided to start reading to see if I could find any other dates when my father went to Jersey. Sure enough there were dates in my scribbled handwriting. I spoke to my counsellor about what to do.

She said, 'It's up to you; you could always telephone the police!'

It played on my mind for a few weeks. I thought that I had nothing to lose and nothing would ever surprise me about my father. I made the call to my local police headquarters in Huntingdon and was transferred to Cambridge headquarters. I gave what information I had, the details about my own abuse, my mother's and my sister Diane's. What stunned me was the police officer saying, 'Why have you not reported this before?'

I was forty-eight years old and didn't have an answer. It was as if someone had just hit me. The officer said he would pass the information on to Jersey police and they would contact me if they needed to. Being given an incident number made it feel very real. I came off the phone and cried, great big sobs; it was just as well no one else was home. All I could think was fucking bastard, why hadn't I reported my own abuse.

This question about reporting abuse is one I have been asked on several occasions. For a long time I didn't even think I'd been abused. It was only as pieces of the puzzle started to fit together that it all made sense. I've always had a feeling that something wasn't quite right with me but I just didn't have the answers. I have them now!

I washed up, I vacuumed and I did my best to clear my mine. It was done now, I'd made the call. The phone rang and I nearly jumped out of my skin, and I felt my heart pounding in my chest. I took a deep breath and picked up the receiver, it was Neil. I let out a huge sigh of relief and told him what I'd done and he said that was good.

When the phone rang again I was ready. The Detective Inspector gave me her name and said she was phoning from Jersey. She asked if I was OK to talk.

'Absolutely,' I replied.

She was kind, sympathetic and professional. The details I gave her were much the same as I'd given to the previous officer. The call was brief and she said she'd call back if she needed anything else. She phoned back within the hour asking if I had a photo of my father from the seventies and any further details. Eventually I was able to get from my brother, my father's passport and a few other older possessions. I scanned the photo into the computer and emailed it across to the Jersey police force. Job done, I thought.

Three weeks passed and I'd heard nothing, so I decided to email. The inspector telephoned me and I waited … She thanked me for the information and I asked the question that had been going round in my head since the last call, 'Did you find anything about my father?'

She said it was highly likely that he had been involved in some sort of paedophilia activities in Jersey, but I have no idea what she may or may not have uncovered. I suppose because he had been dead for over twenty years, they could hardly prosecute him now.

I have other episodes in my diaries about his travels in the UK and abroad during the seventies and eighties. This is one of those questions that I will never have the answers to and to be honest I don't need them. He was on all accounts a paedophile and I know that for a fact.

CHAPTER TWENTY

The Most Perfect Day

My beautiful daughter Hazel on her wedding day in September 2010

Just the five of us – Geoffrey, Hazel, Neil, myself and Graham

Thank you Lizzie for the photograph.

This had to be one of the most memorable and joyful days of my life. I remember the day that Hazel chose her dress and then later changed her mind because she had seen another in a bridal magazine – it did not matter in the slightest. The day was perfect and enjoyed by everyone that attended. Throughout the day my mind wandered back to thoughts of my own wedding and I felt sad, but nothing was going to spoil the happiness of the day that Hazel and Alastair made that commitment to each other.

Written by Ian Currie for me:

> *'Denise remember you are a child of the universe, you have the right to be here, be gentle on yourself'*

CHAPTER TWENTY-ONE

The Year 2011

Friday, May 20th 2011

Today I went to visit my Aunty Betty (mum's sister) and her husband Terry. They live in Enfield in the same house that I stayed in over 30 years ago. This year they will both be eighty. We talked about mum growing up and how they both disliked my father. Terry was the same as I remembered, with the same quick sense of humour. Betty has early Alzheimer's but she was still smiley, slim and well dressed when I went to visit. When I looked at her she just smiled at me, a look that told me she cared.

They had not been in touch for a while with Aunty Gladys (another sister) and gave me her address so I decided to pay her a visit too. My son Graham put the postcode into the Sat Nav and we found her house with ease. Aunty Gladys is eighty-seven years old and has a definite twinkle in her eye, just like my mum; she made me smile. We sat down and had a cup of tea together while she showed me photos of her family, also telling me that she felt there was always something very strange about my father.

She told me her daughter lived next door and she would telephone to see if she was in. She was on the telephone for quite a while and I decided to go and see if she was ok? She handed me the telephone and I heard a man's voice on the other end. I asked him who he was and he replied, 'Who are you?' I told him I was Doreen's daughter. He said he was

Terry (her son) and that her daughter did not in fact live next door. Apparently she believed that everyone lived next door. We made arrangements to speak to each other when I returned from my holiday.

Cyprus June 2011

I have spent my holiday in Cyprus this year writing many of the chapters for this book. It has been not only a mammoth task but also momentous. It has been emotional, bloody difficult and extremely frustrating at times but at the same time a rewarding experience. I still have such a long way to go.

My husband has been extremely patient and I have asked him the same questions over and over again. It has taken a huge amount of courage to ask him for help as this has been something I have always struggled with over the years. I have accepted the constructive criticism from him, but not lightly, because I am so hard on myself due to the many years of being told by my father that I'm stupid, thick and useless.

When reliving the past and writing it down in my own words I have been transported back in time. This has been horrendous, useful and paramount to the book. Having the space and peace to write in a beautiful setting with no interruptions has been a key factor for me. Though I must say towards the end of our vacation some very noisy insects made it very difficult for me concentrate. I would get so pissed off that I'd stop to take a break and decided to sit outside, but it wasn't long before I came back inside because I couldn't stand the noise.

Writing a book about my life has been an ambition of mine for so long that I've lost count of how many times I've said I wanted to do it. Tracking down older family members has highlighted my own mortality and how easy they have forgotten dates and times of significant events. It would certainly have been a lot easier not to write the book. However, I am fortunate that I kept my diaries for so long as the information they hold has been invaluable.

I have learnt things about myself that I didn't know. Firstly I would not confess to being a writer but I have written this. I have learnt I am brutally honest and do not dress things up. What you see is what you get with me. I hope my humour has come through in my writing as being able to laugh at one's self I believe is truly the best medicine.

I am determined that this book shall be published for it is an account of the terrible truths that I have witnessed and been a survivor of. I am a testament to any other person who has an untold story and who is umming and arring about what to do – I say just go for it. If I'm not successful in finding a publisher then I shall publish the book myself – the story will be told.

As I look back and think about my life today I am blessed. I have a wonderful husband and three amazing children, each of whom have special partners. I have a sister who is my best friend and confidante. There are a handful of people in my life now with whom I choose to share my most precious thoughts, people who I know will not ridicule or laugh at me. I am accepted for who I truly am. I make no apologies for the content in this book however distasteful it may seem.

My belief is that I chose the parents that I had because I had some valuable lessons to learn about myself. It is this belief that keeps me strong in the knowledge that next time when my soul is ready to move into another human being for transport, I shall choose again. My spiritual journey has many years to travel and I have other lessons to learn yet. The soul is, I believe ageless and sexless, we reap what we sow and what goes around comes around. I treat others with respect and kindness even if I don't always agree with what they say. For now I am at total peace, in this ever-changing world of possessions and greed and know how easy it is to miss the most important thing of all. There is only one thing that we can be sure of and that is this moment in time, for true happiness comes from within and tomorrow never comes.

Life is difficult

This is a great truth, one of the greatest truths.

> *It is a great truth because once we truly see this truth, we transcend it. Once we truly know that life is difficult – once we truly understand and accept it – then life is no longer difficult. Because once it is accepted, the fact that life is difficult no longer matters.*

The book, *The Road Less Travelled* by M. Scott Peck was given to me by my sister Mandy many years ago and helps us to explore the nature of loving relationships. It teaches us to become less dependent and yet become more sensitive to those around us, but ultimately how to accept one's true self.

December 2011

My mothers General hospital notes arrive and it is Saturday morning. I have waited and waited for this day to arrive. The anticipation of what I may or may not discover is over whelming. The white envelope is large and heavy, there just has to be something about me in all that stuff. And there I am listed with my siblings in chronological order in the Ante Natal Records.

Home term normal throughout. 6lb 6oz breast fed.

This new information brings me to tears, I have waited fifty-two years for this. I weep and my husband holds me, at last I have some acknowledgement of my birth and my weight. I look at it once and then again just to make sure I'm seeing the words correctly. This is the very best Christmas present ever, well actually I'd love to find the little dolly from years ago but that would be just too good to be true.

* * * * *

Aunty Gladys passed away on Wednesday, 12th May 2012, she was eighty-eight years old.

Aunty Gladys's is my mother's eldest sister and Terry is her son. My husband and I met Terry and his wife Irene before the funeral in Hertford. They gave me some photos of my mother that I had never seen before and I was emotional and touched by their kindness. We shared a lunch together and I felt like I belonged to this family for the very first time in my life. When we were ready to leave Neil and I decided to go home via the cemetery where my mother was buried. Terry bought flowers for my mothers grave, I said I would tell her they were from him and of course I did as I lay them in front of her grave stone.

Aunty Gladys' funeral was how I believe a funeral should be a celebration of a life. I was fortunate to also meet my mother's elder brother, John, who looked remarkably like my mother with very similar mannerisms to her. I made arrangements to go to my uncle John's and his wife's home the following week. They promised they would sort some old photographs out for me to look at. I felt a strange sense of belonging that afternoon as other family members commented on my likeness to the Nott family.

Later in the year Terry and Irene came to our cottage for the day. Terry once again gave me a selection of photographs, some of the house that my mother was born in and others. Terry is younger than my mother and it's clear from the photos that she was like a big sister to him and that he was very fond of her. He spoke with great affection towards her. I have been surprised by Terry's generosity, he has offered to help me in any way with the publication of my book and this has made me feel like for the first time I have a brother's support even though he is not my brother.

CHAPTER TWENTY-TWO

The Road to Recovery and What's in a Dream?

The dream that follows has been an occurring lucid dream for as long as I can remember. It is this dream that led me to start working with dream therapy.

> *I hear the familiar sound of the front door closing, am I asleep or awake, I'm not sure? I hear footsteps coming up the stairs and clicking knees, I know you are there, I sense you. My heart is pounding in my chest, so fast and loud, I'm sure you can hear it. I am lying still in the bed unable to move, not daring to breathe. Locked in a lucid dream. A flashback. 'Keep still, don't move' I tell myself. Then the covers move slightly, the weight of you makes the bed sink. You are on top of me moving. How do I know what is going on for I am just a child...*

All the dreams that follow have been recorded as they were dreamt. I have removed some names and replaced with the word sibling so as not to offend or upset anyone

Monday, October 8th 2007

It was dark and I was frightened, I could not see because the electricity had just run out and I was waiting to see if dad would put a tanner (sixpence) in the meter. The

bed and room were messy. My sister was in the bed too. I started to take my clothes off.

Tuesday, October 9th 2007

My sister had given me an alcoholic drink and then I had been given three tablets. I would soon be asleep; I needed to drink lots of water. The ambulance would soon arrive.

Collecting rocks and stones in a wheelbarrow, someone was kissing my neck. I noticed all the stones were different. Dad was watching...

Monday, October 15th 2007

I was in that house, number 56, dad had gone out. There was only a dry stale loaf of bread to eat so I made it wet. I went out with two ladies to buy a loaf of bread. We came to a nice shop but they said the bread was horrid. I thought it was ok. Then I was upstairs at 56. Neil said he had had enough of me behaving like this, he looked angry. I went into the bathroom to look for my toiletry bag. There were lots of bags all packed, so I took mine and kicked a pile of suitcases over as I went back into the room. In my bag there were earplugs and hearing aids. I was then in bed, with a tent like thing over me like a roof. The sun had gone in and there was water all around. Part of my mouth came out, it was like a gum shield and it looked horrid. I thought how am I going to get up and how am I going to hide this? I tried to get it back into my mouth but I started to gag and choke. I woke up.

Tuesday, October 23rd 2007

I was in the back of my car; it was dark and I was frightened. I did not want to get out. I thought I was locking the door but unlocked it instead. Then these hands were coming for me, I screamed 'NO' and woke up...

Thursday, October 25th 2007

A child was lying on the floor and they were being hit and told they would be killed. I had just arrived home. Someone was upstairs, an intruder. A small, young girl came down the stairs. I rang the police but they let her go. She had already been in the house earlier and stolen all my jewellery and possessions, I was so upset.

Sunday, October 28th 2007

I was standing in the doorway to a dark room. The room was untidy and unkempt. The curtains were drawn and on the bed were two capsules lying in a piece of crumpled foil. Dad was moaning and angry. He started ripping up a folder of work that had lovely drawings in it and I shouted at him to stop. I said, 'You cannot do that, a lot of hard work and effort has been put into that'. A brother then came into the room and also told him to stop it.

Saturday, November 3rd 2007

Surrounded by rivers I was with two old school friends. We were going for a walk but I was not quite ready. We sat for a while then continued our walk. I was then at home again but realised I had left the pram behind, it was a big double Silver Cross pram, but then I remembered that we did not actually need it any more. I got up and picked up my shoes as well as two pairs of children's shoes that were wet. I emptied the water out and gave them to the children. Then as if I was dreaming in my dream, I was being held onto by someone. It wasn't frightening, I felt sort of safe and then we began to roll over. I was holding on tightly. I was aware something was in my mouth but I am not quite sure what. I could then feel the semen in my mouth and the movement. I woke up and I felt disgusting.

Wednesday, November 14th 2007

I was very young and being chased by two men outside the railway station. The station was just as I had remembered it over forty years ago. I was very high up just out of their reach. It was autumn, they could not quite catch me. I was frightened.

Thursday, November 15th 2007

In a house the television was on, people were talking about paedophiles. They said, 'He should not be allowed to stand next to little girls'. I said, 'He would like that'. They showed a picture of my dad on the screen, it was horrid. I said, "I do not want to look at it,' and walked away.

There was a large cinema screen and there were words coming out saying, 'Tapping had been heard from outer space' and that something was coming to earth. I could see from the window people digging trenches. I was lying down naked and I tried to cover myself. As I lay there hands were coming towards me going around my throat. I stopped fighting and lay still. I was trying to explain to people what had happened. Nobody else seemed scared; they just accepted what had happened.

Friday, November 16th 2007

Outside in the street, it was dark and there were lots of men dressed in dark clothing. They were scruffy. They were all around me. One man said, 'I was lovely'. I knew I needed to get away, so I said 'Thank you' as I did not want to antagonise him. I was then in the living room of number 56 and dad was cleaning the fireplace, while I stood there watching him.

Tuesday, November 20th 2007

We were all sitting around the tables at 56 ready to have a meal. I sat with my elder brother and sister while the others sat on another table. I got up and kissed Diane and then kissed another sister, she looked sad.

Friday, November 24th 2007

Flashback

Standing in the hall in my home looking out the window I am forty eight years old, it was dark and as I turned there he was, dad just standing and staring at me.

Friday, November 24th 2007

It was night time, I was upstairs and wanted to catch dad out, to see what he was up to!! All the doors were closed. I crept slowly down the stairs opened the living room door quickly, but only two boys were in there, not dad. I suddenly realised he was actually upstairs in one of the rooms. I woke up.

The funeral was about to begin, I was getting ready with a lady. (I did not know her.) We thought we would be late as they were all just about to leave. We went up the stairs; the house was really nice not at all what I expected. In the kitchen the units were made of wood with red trim around the edges. It was clean and tidy. There were lots of children around. I needed to take my shoes off because I did not like them. I had no tights on just bare feet. I thought, 'Oh well who cares'. I saw an old friend, he was lovely to me. I missed him.

Monday, November 27th 2007

I am at 56 and I am coming down from upstairs into the kitchen. Someone had just gone out the back door. I called them back. I said, 'Please come back'. I was not angry or frightened. I think they had been washing clothes, and then I noticed it was getting lighter outside. A voice said, 'They had been washing clothes for four years'. I looked out of the window and saw that it had been snowing, I was so excited.

I was in the kitchen at 56 and a few other people were there. On some of the cupboards there were white spots. I heard them say they did not know how they got there. A man from work showed me into the next room and there were more spots. I said to him, 'You did it' and he said, 'I did not'. Then I said, 'Yes you did, I can tell'. He started to laugh. On the side there were different boxes of glue all leaking. The glue was on my hands and I could not get it off.

Saturday, December 8th 2007

Dad had hold of me and I could not get away. I was trying to fight him off; he just seemed to be everywhere. Then I was walking with a brother, trying to tell him what had happened.

The lady was baking outside. She was sitting down and the oven was in front of her. There was a queue of people in front of her and I was one of the last in the queue. I did not want to push in. When it was my turn the lady gave me a bowl, flour, eggs and milk. I mixed them up, and although it took a little while she did not hurry me. When it was well mixed and smooth her husband appeared and I told him that I sometimes put four eggs in but it did not always turn out right. I poured the mixture into a tin. The lady was getting ready to leave and the door closed. I needed to pay her; I was worried that I did not have enough money. As I went through my bag I dropped some things. I gave her fifteen pounds in notes.

Monday, December 11th 2007

This dream was very upsetting and I had woken up crying.

A very close relative had died and a young baby was now without their mother. I saw a sister and she did not seem upset. I told her the relative had died because of the operation. I could see the blood, it was a large blob in the corner of the room and it was getting bigger and bigger. With no warning it burst and the blood went everywhere. I still could not believe she had died. I was then in my bedroom at 56. I was trying to ring a friend but the phone was not working. I pulled out the cable connection and put it back in. I could hear voices, so I disconnected it. My friend then appeared in the room and I told her about my relative dying. She did not seem bothered about it at all.

Monday, December 10th 2007

I was walking along an overgrown path to Old Welwyn. I could feel someone behind me and as I turned round I saw dad coming along on a motorbike. The bike kept stopping and starting. I was a little way ahead of him on the path and I felt scared. I was trying to get away.

I had not seen my mum for weeks as I had been away. In 56 I asked my sister when she had seen mum last. She replied, 'Twenty-one days ago' and I was horrified that no one seemed concerned. I then realised she was missing. I just knew dad had done something to her. (I felt sick) I started to ask him what he had done to her.

He said he had murdered her. I asked him where she was and he told me she was in St Mary's cemetery. He had buried her. I went into the other room and knelt down in front of my elder brother and sister and told them that he had killed mum. They said they did not believe me. It did not matter because I knew where she was. Dad was lying down and I stroked his head and he told me it was good to confess. We then went out into the garden and I could see quite along way in the distance. The cemetery was at the bottom of the garden. Dad was looking and I sensed he felt uncomfortable. Back indoors I was aware my hair was wet and wrapped in a towel. I took the towel off. In the bathroom I quietly said to my brother I did not want to sleep on my own, but I could not sleep with him. I was scared that I would also be murdered in my sleep.

Friday, January 3rd 2008

Sitting with my father, he said he had a book to show me. I asked him what it was about. He replied that it was a very old book and that he had had it a long time. He told me it was full of all sorts of pictures of people doing things to each other. Things that were not very nice, not very nice at all he said. I woke up.

Saturday January 4th 2008

In this dream I was half-lying and half-sitting up on the sofa, I had a night dress on. Dad was next to me. I was aware no one else was in the room. He moved closer to me and put his finger into my bottom, I flinched and told him that it really hurt. He was looking at me and smiling as he pushed his finger in further. I lay very still for a moment. I was then aware that I was getting up and running out of the room. I had no shoes on. I then was knocking at a neighbour's door and said that I wanted to speak to the lady that lived in the house. She wasn't in, but there were other children there. I couldn't tell anyone what had just happened. I saw my elder sister and said I was going to tell the police, she asked 'Why?' I hated her and was so upset. Then I was near the sea and could see two young girls close to the edge. The waves were splashing up and I was concerned for their well-being. I placed my hand on one of the girl's shoulders and noticed that her mother was looking at me strangely; she gave me such a glare. I moved away. I returned a few minuets later only to find one of the girls had fallen over the edge and the other girl was holding onto her. She was clinging on with all her might; I managed to pull her up and she was safe.

Tuesday, January 8th 2008

As I was sitting in the living room at 56 and watching the television, I could see a man watching me through the window. He looked at me and I looked at him. As I got up to move, he moved too and followed me, but from outside. I started to close the curtains.

Thursday, January 10th 2008

The couple over the road had a new baby girl. My sister Diane was with me in the house. From where I stood I could see next door's bathroom window. The light was shining through and on the windowsill I could see

Johnson's baby lotion and baby bath. I walked into our kitchen and looking out the window I saw a pram with a baby boy inside. I knew it was not the baby from the neighbour's house because it was a boy. Someone must have put him there to sleep and the noises coming from our house had settled him. I said to Diane to come and look but when I looked again he had disappeared. Diane was standing there holding him. I said 'Put him back before someone notices'. She said, 'No'. I then physically moved her and then noticed the pram had vanished. We then found ourselves outside with the police; there was a lady with the empty pram. She came over and took the baby back. People were saying that Diane was not at all well.

I was being chased through the rooms of 56. I ran up the stairs into the bathroom, I was trying to shut and lock the door. It would not lock and I just about had time to get out the window. It was dark outside and I knew he was following me. People were walking. I could not see him but I sensed he was there. I was then in a shopping centre. I saw three plastic containers, one yellow and two red, which were all filled with strawberries covered in sugar. I ate one and it did not taste of anything.

Friday, January 18th 2008

Being chased in 56. It was dark and I ran up the stairs. I was hiding behind the bathroom door. I was peeping out the gap between the hinges. Dad was there. I had nowhere to hide...

Saturday, January 19th 2008

I was with a really nice, kind man. He told me he would buy me a morning coat. We arrived at an expensive shop and two ladies came out and took me into a small room. The light came on. I was worried that I would have to take my clothes off because they needed to measure me. I did not need to; they said they knew my size. We left the shop. On top of the bags were little gifts, earrings; I was very happy.

Lying down a man was touching me. I was trying so hard to get away but he was much stronger than me. I was so frightened. Then I was in a garden, looking over the fence, and I could see a mound of earth. A cat sat at the entrance with its back to me. A short fat man came out of the house who looked a little like my father, but it was not him. He was looking at the mound of earth which also looked a little like a temple.

In another room I was with a sister when three men came in. I thought to myself, 'I am not happy with this'. One of the men left the room through an open door and I made a dash for the door too.

I had started a new job and was waiting in a queue; I was holding two tea cups. It was my job to get the tea. There were so many tea cups, they were everywhere. The queue was so long and there were lots of different people. In front of me was a man and I was aware that I was leaning on him, probably because I knew I had to wait a long time. The man in front of me put his hand up my skirt and I tried to pull my petticoat down. He was young and strong and I felt the urge to touch his back, but I did not. I was once again in the queue and now most of the people had gone. For a while I could not find my cups. When I finally found my cups I made some tea.

Friday, February 8th 2008

I was pretending to be asleep (dreaming) and someone was really close to my face. I shouted at them to get away from me, to leave me alone. But every time I moved my face away he was there. I woke up in the dream, upset and crying.

This type of nightmare is always particularly upsetting, especially as I wake crying real tears. It messes me up for days because it is so real.

Standing at the top of the stairs at 56, dad was at the bottom of the stairs smoking and he had also been drinking. I was shouting at him. Telling him smoking and drinking was no good for him. I hated him.

I was climbing up a muddy, rocky slope. I was with someone else and we were pulling something else. We climbed a little way, and something was holding onto me. I thought that was OK just keep going.

Saturday, February 9th 2008

I was looking after some of my siblings at 56. One of my sisters was doing her homework but she wanted to go out to play and kept getting up to go. I called her back several times and told her she must finish the work first. Two other sisters were in the downstairs toilet and they were washing underwear in the tiny sink. I asked if everything was OK. One sister said that she kept wetting herself and the underwear was now stained. I asked her how old she was and she started counting 8, 9, 10 and 11. I was going to explain about periods, but then we were outside walking. There was another girl there who I was also taking care of. She said she did not feel very well and was suddenly vomiting. I tried so hard to get her to a sink but it was too late. She had vomited up clots of blood and I asked her how long had it been going on. She said that it happened all the time. A lady arrived and asked me how I had been getting on; I told her everything was fine but asked her why she not told me the girl had a medical condition. We then started to clean the blood up with tissues.

Tuesday, February 12th 2008

In this dream I was in an unknown house. A man was coming to visit. When the man arrived he was walking slowly and managed to get up the stairs. He stayed one night but the following morning he said he would like to stay another night, then he came over to me and said goodbye. He bent over and was very close, he was pushing himself up against me and he had an erection which I could feel through his coat. I shouted at him saying he could not stay. I ran up the stairs and sat on the bed. The room was small with purple curtains and a bedspread that matched. The window was tiny. I noticed the covers were pulled back a little and I sat there waiting for someone to come. There had been a women, I did not know who she was. I was going to tell her everything. No one came.

Thursday, February 14th 2008

I was in a bedroom with some other children. A little boy about two years old was looking for clothes. He started to put shorts and short socks on and I was thinking that the clothes were not appropriate at all for the time of year. I needed to find him some other clothes. I kissed him on the forehead and told him he was lovely. I was aware that I was just a few months pregnant and I felt sad that they did not have enough clothes.

This morning after my husband had gone to work I laid in bed for a while.

The nightmare begins…

I hear the front door close, the footsteps on the stairs. The stillness of the silence and my heart pounding in my chest. I sense the movement of him as he enters my bedroom. The covers are moving, I feel hands around my ankles and I am being pulled into a position I don't want to be in. I was trying to move away. I thought, if I just peep out through my eyes I could see who it was. He was on the other side of the bed now. The covers were being lifted lightly and slowly. I was trying, fighting to wake up. I did wake up or so I thought, but I was still dreaming. I am frozen, hardly able to breathe, trying so hard not to make a sound. I feel his hands touching me. He is on top of me and raping me. I keep my eyes closed tightly.

I was walking at the Mimram, a river fairly close to where I live. The bridge over the river did not look safe. It started to collapse. There were children and adults standing on the bridge. The water was running fast and I could see the water rising and starting to flood where some of the children were standing. I shouted to the adults, telling them it was dangerous. They asked me how I knew and I replied I had been walking there for twenty-eight years.

Monday, February 18th 2008

I am sitting with my sister Diane in the living room at 56. Dad was holding a drink of whisky. As he went through the door I said to my sister, 'He is always like this when he has had a drink'. He turned around and said, 'What did you say?' I said, 'Nothing'. I watched his shadow as it went up the stairs, just to make sure he had gone. I got up and went into the kitchen. On the side was a half bottle of red wine. I walked back through the hall way and there were lots of people. A lady was sitting on a chair crying and I asked her what was wrong; she said we could not talk there so we went up to my room where it was quieter. We went up the stairs.

My room was not where it usually was, there were three different beds in there. I went to the next bedroom and that was not mine either. I asked someone where my room was and all my things. I could see my bed had been dismantled and was standing up against the wall in the corner on the landing. I was desperately upset and crying. I shouted, 'Where's dad?' and went downstairs to find him. I then had a cup of tea in my hand. I could see my dad, he looked young, he was looking at me with a shocked expression on his face. I threw the tea over him and started shouting at him, but he just started to laugh. I pushed him and we fell onto the floor. He felt strong and young. I was hitting his face trying hard to hurt him. I held a knife and the look on his face was one of fright. Throwing the knife down I yelled at him saying I was going to tell everyone what he had done to me and what he had been doing.

Tuesday, February 19th 2008

I dreamt I was working in a funeral directors. I needed to staple some papers together but I stapled them into my left palm instead. I then had to pull them out. My hand was swollen, bruised and bleeding. All I wanted to do was get things right.

Friday, February 22nd 2008

I was at the house in Knightsfield where I was born. There was a little girl there and I lifted her up onto a wall, or it could have been a side. I told her I would only be a few minutes and went off to the shops. I had a key to open the shop door and once inside I started looking for something (I was not sure what). My mother was next to me and she spoke just a few words, but I do not remember what they were.

Sunday, February 24th 2008

In this dream I was at school. I needed to go and buy two new short-sleeved, white tops. The tops were in packets of two and they were priced at five pounds. When I arrived at the till the lady said that the cost would be over five thousand pounds. I said, 'How come?' She replied, 'They are really expensive'. I left the shop and realised that I was holding a pair of trousers. I went back into the shop and apologised to the lady and asked her how much the trousers were, she said, 'Forty-two pounds'. I bought them. I was then telling people at school how expensive the shirts were. I was given some work to do on three cards, it was homework. I needed to prepare for tomorrow.

Saturday, March 1st 2008

I had to go and help in a school. I could not remember how to get to class five. I asked a male teacher and he looked heavenwards and said, 'It's that way'. I went into a building but I could not see properly. I went up some stairs and came to class five which was on my left. I could hear that registration had already started, so I knocked and went in. I was greeted by the class teacher and we shook hands. In the class there were three other adults, one male and two females. The other male teacher came up to me and said hello. I thought he was going to shake my hand but instead the hand went behind me. It felt like the hand was going into my bottom. It hurt and I asked him to stop. The look he gave me was as if he was saying, 'What's wrong, I always do that'. (Someone had already told me he liked bottoms.) I then went to say hello to each child. I sat on the floor with my legs crossed. One by one I spoke to each child telling them my name. Once I had done this I had to climb onto a really high chair so that I was sitting with the teachers. I fell off and had to climb up again. One of the teachers was reading a book and translating from Russian to English.

I was in a National Trust house and part of the house was a Laura Ashley shop. A lady came into the shop to return some curtains that had started to fall to pieces. I said I would get the manager to sort it out and asked the lady to wait. I went to find the manager but kept getting lost. I saw a lady I used to work with, with her husband. She said hello to me and we walked together for a while. Then I was outside and realising this I knew I would not be able to get back in as I would need my swipe card. I decided to try and get in anyway. Standing in the queue I could see a lady lying down having an epileptic fit. I was thinking someone should be supporting her head. I saw that the doors were closed and the curtains were drawn.

Thursday, March 6th 2008

I have woken with a headache after a long interrupted night; I dreamt loads but can't seem to remember much.

In this dream I was in a small house. I was aware there were lots of people around. The house was dark, messy and very busy. I had to go into the garden. I could see a small patch of green grass. There was also a tree. The ground was messy, wet and damp. I was caught up in the washing line. A man came out and I asked him if it would be ok if I cut the washing line. He said it would be alright and I then started cutting it with my teeth.

Saturday, March 8th 2008

Once again I am in a house. Upstairs people are sorting clothes and putting them into black bags. My husband was taking some stuff. I decided to go downstairs because I did not want to do it. Everyone seemed to be organised. Downstairs was just like a pub. I went outside into the garden; it was good to be out in the fresh air. There were people walking and some were sitting drinking. I knew that my husband would wonder where I was, but I did not really care. When I eventually decided to come back I had to cut through a pub. I walk for a while and then went in through the door. There were people everywhere and it was very smoky. A man came up to me and he said he would like to be with me. He was a nuisance and I ignored him. I could see tables and chairs. I was then outside walking again and came to a very expensive hotel. Inside the hotel I saw a man who was dressed in

Beefeater clothes and they were coloured green. I then saw my husband coming out of another hotel; he said to me, 'I have been worried about you and looking for you'. I replied, 'I have just been for a walk'.

Thursday, March 13th 2008

I was walking on my way home to 56 when I heard a sister's voice. I went to her and said, 'Hello'. She told me she would be home in a moment so I carried on towards the house but as I got closer it became darker. I was aware there were no street lights. I was frightened and I looked around. As I approached the house I saw two vans parked outside. A man was ripping posters from the car window. I went inside. I could hear music playing and did not like it. Dad was there and ignoring me. I asked him why he was just wearing underpants and socks. He said he was dressed for the weather. The music was playing and I shut the door. I went upstairs and my sister was there who was also not dressed properly. I told her to go into the other room and use her own bathroom and toilet. I said to her that is why we bought the house because it has separate bathrooms. She looked at me and started to cry.

Saturday, March 15th 2008

I was walking home and could hear my sister's voice and I started to walk towards it. She was with some friends of hers and they were laughing. I asked her if she was coming home and she replied, 'In a minute'. I carried on walking towards 56 and as I got closer to the house it started to get darker and darker. I realised the street lamps weren't working and I felt frightened because I sensed someone was there. When I arrived at the house I could see two vans outside. A man was taking posters off it. I went inside. My sister was upstairs. I said to her to use the other bathroom. That's why we bought the house, for more space. All the rooms were lovely.

In this dream I was walking home to 56. I was carrying a handbag, coat and another bag. I crossed the road to avoid a man who I didn't like the look of but he started to come towards me so I shouted at him. I had then taken a different route and soon realised I'd gone a long way out of my way. I tried to ring Neil to pick me up but I couldn't work the telephone. There was a red phone box so I went in. I could see a black man standing at the door. I was frightened and dropped all of my things. I quickly picked them up and ran out but realised I had left my bag behind. The man had tipped everything out. I wanted my bag and so I went back. I took my purse and then ran. I could see a house and the lights were on. In the garden I could see tin cans and so much rubbish. I decided to go to the house next door. I knocked on the door and a lady answered. I told her I needed her to ring the police because someone had stolen my bag. She said, 'Ok'. I asked her if I could sit on the floor which was made of lino. I saw shoes, bags and there were coats hanging up. The front door was glass and I could still see the man in the phone box. She said she needed to go and make the children's tea and left me sitting there.

Friday, March 28th 2008

I was sitting in the living room at 56. A sister sat opposite and she looked lovely. I asked her if she was ok and she said, 'Yes'. Two younger sisters got up to go to the toilet, followed by dad. I knew he was going to do something to them; he had that strange look on his face. I then got up to follow; I was going to spy on him. I was aware someone else had also got up, so I decided not to go.

I was then with Sharon and we were looking at some old stuff. Wrapped in tissue paper was a piece of white lace; it was delicate and beautifully made but it was unfinished. On the lace was my father's name, but the last letter was missing. I asked my sister where it had come from and she said a relative of dad's had made it. There was also a bracelet, which was also wrapped. Sharon wouldn't look at it because she said dad used to wear it. I was thinking it was a very feminine bracelet because it had coloured beads on it and ribbons.

Sunday, March 30th 2008

I dreamt I was in a church. There were lots of activities going on such as painting, drawing and reading. I could see many people. A man came to me and said how lovely the children were and the references that they were making about the church. I told him the children were not mine. I said my own children were much older. As we were leaving and saying goodbye, we hugged and kissed different people. The chap in charge was a man I'd met last year at a course I attended. We said goodbye to each other and hugged, but he wouldn't let me go. We fell over together, it was quite funny. Once outside I knew I had to get to the train station, there wasn't much time so I had to hurry. The pushchair that my little boy was in wasn't working properly; I needed to get a new one. I was conscious of the time.

I was walking backwards towards 56. The house looked different, more space somehow. There was a man following me so I moved quickly, turning into our pathway that led to the house. I felt scared and panicky. I rushed along the alleyway and opened the back door. I shouted to my dad that a man was after me. I needed to lock the back door but I struggled to find the correct key; it was number nine. I locked the door just in time as the man shouted. I hid quickly behind the dining room door. As I peeped through the crack dad answered the door. The man asked if I was indecent and they started to have an in-depth conversation.

Saturday, April 5th 2008

I was aware there were lots of family members around. Some of us were waiting for a concert to start. We were going to watch it on a small screen so we turned it around to the right so everyone could see. A friend of mine arrived and I told her it was really expensive, about one thousand pounds. Her hair was messy and she had a skirt that she needed to put over her trousers; they would then know she was female. A few other members of the family arrived. I was really pleased they had come and they sat down. I was sitting on a chair and next to me was a male member of our family, he sat on my right. He whispered in my ear saying that he would be there for me today, tomorrow and the next day. I kept quiet. I was aware I could hear Neil. I could see he was going into a dark room so I got up to go and listen but just as I got to there, there was a loud noise. People were thinking that I'd said something to him and it was my fault. I told them he had thrown a book down and had missed the chair. The people in the room were waiting for the music to start. Neil had been drinking and I came away. I was then walking with Diane. I said to Diane, 'I've made my mind up that I will leave'. Ian was upset but Diane said I could move in.

Away to Grenada April 2008
Working as a volunteer with the leather back turtles.

Monday, May 12th 2008

In this dream I just remember being in a house. Someone was outside. I needed to close the windows and lock the doors to stop them getting in. I was frightened.

The window in this dream signifies that I am trying to deal with my inner feelings and needing to escape from something.

Tuesday, May 13th 2008

I dreamt someone was there. They said to me that I didn't need to see them to know they were there. I was calling for my brother...

I woke from this dream, scared, frightened and alone.

Saturday, May 17th 2008

I was attending a university or college. I was counting tiny squares and placing them in the correct place, then filing them. Then I was pushing a lady in a pram/pushchair. I was aware there were lots of people around, a beautiful building and a purple wisteria growing up the building which wasn't yet in full bloom. The lady climbed out of the pushchair thing and it turned into a wheelbarrow, but I carried on pushing it.

Sunday, May 18th 2008

In this dream I was in a hospital/doctor's surgery. I was dressed in over clothes. I went to speak to the receptionist and asked to see a doctor. I told her it was about my left hand which had a large gash in it. As I stood there a large blob of stuff came out of the gash and I just stared down at it. The lady at the desk covered it over.

Monday, May 26th 2008

Dreaming about elephants ... I was in a car with two other ladies. One lady was driving. It was raining and very muddy. The lady driving said if she drives slowly the elephants will be ok. If they should get cross they will charge. A large male started to come towards us and the lady was driving faster now. I was thinking to myself that she obviously knows the road and what to do.

Elephants in a dream are to recognise the qualities of patience, long memory, strength and fidelity. In the more esoteric sense it signifies radiant and glowing wisdom

Saturday, May 31st 2008

I dreamt I was planting bulbs and some of them had already started to grow. I was sleeping at night in a field at the bottom of a hill and was next to a fence. Two men offered me some cheese, but I said no thank you. I was thinking that they didn't speak any English. I had to then go to the top of the hill to take a shower. I could also see a red van. Around me was a really large black wrap.

Sunday, June 1st 2008

I was dreaming a lucid dream…

I was aware someone had thrown some sort of liquid over and onto my left shoulder. I wiped it off. I was then aware it was dry!! It was semen and my father was standing next to me.

This made me feel sick!!

Monday, June 2nd 2008

I and my immediate family were all boarding a ship. The ship was huge and the waves enormous. I was worried about our youngest son and asked my husband to go and get him. I was then in a shop which sold baby and children's clothes. My daughter was about three years old. I was looking for pink tights. I asked my son if he needed anything and we started to look at trousers.

I dreamt someone had hold of me. I couldn't get away. I was at 56 in the kitchen.

Monday, June 9th 2008

This dream was once again at 56. I was the age I am now forty-nine. My husband had died, but he was also there but not as my husband. The bed was empty and I started to cry. I spoke to my eldest son about insurance and he said he would be able to help me. My other son was there and I had to tell him what had happened. I sat with him and put my arm around him. I told him I had something to tell him. I said there were only four of us now and told him dad had passed away.

I was inside a house and I'd said to my daughter she could take a few of my personal belongings from the glass cabinet. I noticed that she had taken a lot more of my favourite things and I was upset. I started to tell her what she'd taken.

I was then outside, to my left there was a man-made river, which was going uphill. I could see some people watching green turtles as they swam up the river. I started to explain to them about the time I had spent in Grenada with turtles.

In a house again I saw my cat. She is a beautiful black cat. I had a hot cup of tea and she caught her leg in it. The hot tea went all over her tummy. I wasn't able to catch her. Someone was saying she needed to go to the vets.

Friday, June 13th 2008

I'd gone to visit my parents in their house 56. There was stuff everywhere. Dad came down the stairs, he had shorts on and his left foot was missing. I wondered how I'd never noticed it before. Mum had lost weight and she was busy tidying up. There were four children and a little boy of about three years old came and sat next to me on my left. I put my arm around him and he started asking questions, after a short time he fell asleep. Mum said, 'Good another one's asleep'. Someone knocked at the front door, it was a delivery man with some medication which mum signed for. She was putting it with some other medication into a locked first aid cupboard in the downstair's loo. I was telling them both about my new job and trip. Mum went off and dad said to me, 'Be careful'.

I went into another room but felt I could still be seen. I was washing my hair and my body. He was watching me, but he could only see above my shoulders or so I thought. I covered myself up. I hadn't washed all the shampoo out and was trying to comb it out. I got up to find my clothes, jeans, top, bra and knickers. I asked my dad where the toilet was because I needed to get dressed. I was now in the hallway and could see through the glass front door. I said I didn't realise there was so much space.

I was again in the living room and sitting on the settee with dad next to me and it felt nice. Mum was coming down the stairs and he moved away.

During this dream I was aware I was sitting on a double bed. I thought it was strange that the bed was downstairs. Under the covers I could see a hole in the bed and thought, this is the bed mum and dad sleep in.

To dream of dead people that we have known (both my parents) usually refers back to strong emotions, whether they are negative or positive. Memories can remain buried for years and often when we dream of dead people that we have known we are being reminded of different times, which then helps us to deal with the present.

Tuesday, June 17th 2008

Dad was angry. He was hitting my brothers and sisters, punching them and shouting... The children were all crying. I was comforting one of my younger brothers as he was small, only about ten months old. I said to another sister that I was thinking of reporting him to the social services. She pulled a face. I said I just didn't know what else to do. I told her, 'Next time he hits anyone I'm going to say to him, "I'm going to report you".' I was thinking to myself it would be better if he'd had a drink, then he would be calmer to start with and not so violent. Dad was then going outside to light some fireworks. I stayed inside to comfort two younger sisters.

In this dream couples were dancing and they were all dressed the same. I was going into a school; I could see two other girls and they asked me if I had the work ready. I said, 'No, I didn't think I needed it'. They went into the classroom. I decided to go in, but did not sit near them. I could still hear what they were saying, they were talking about how I cooked chips.

It was night time and a younger sister was also with me. She told me she was leaving and I could go with her. I went to get my car. I had to walk along a long path to get to the car park. A man was behind me and then he was at my side. He started talking about my vagina. He kept on and on. I didn't like him and I pushed him away. My car wasn't in the car park which meant I had to walk back. The man was now on the opposite side of the fence.

I was in a house with my daughter and husband. Our cat came into the room and she had been mutilated (my husbands words). Half her back was missing and she was crawling on the floor and bleeding. I looked and most of her insides were missing. She also had diarrhoea. I thought she would die at any moment. I asked if I should call the vet because she is suffering. Then she got up, not completely fine, but I was stroking her. She wasn't purring.

Thursday, July 3rd 2008

I went into the front room of a house, the rooms were large. I thought it was strange that the door was unlocked. Inside it was very quiet. I could feel someone was there, but I didn't see them. I moved through the rooms and came to the bathroom. I opened the door and just behind the door was the toilet. As I closed the door the toilet was flushed so I knew someone was there. I ran for the door to get away, I wasn't quick enough...

Later I said to my husband that the door was locked and I couldn't find the key. He said, 'Look it's here'. It had been hung in the wrong place. I told him a man had been in the house and that I was frightened.

Keys in a dream

They represent fresh attitudes, thoughts and feelings which are capable of unlocking memories, experiences and knowledge which we have previously hidden.

In this dream I was working and a lady gave me some powdered stuff in two bags. I said I couldn't accept it because it had no labels on it. I asked a man who I knew if that was right and he said 'Yes'. The lady came back with the labels and they stuck to the surface. I then had trouble getting them off. I was aware there were quite a few men around and they were making a fuss of me. I told them the only person I was interested in was the guy there who I knew.

Wednesday, July 9th 2008

I was dreaming I was in a housing estate. I had to climb up some steep concrete steps and hold onto a pole. I was carrying a small child (a girl) who was about two years old and wearing a nappy. I didn't think I would be able to make it and couldn't understand why Neil wouldn't carry her. I needed to change her nappy, so I looked for a toilet. There didn't seem to be any way out, just the steep steps.

Friday, July 11th 2008

I was walking outside and it was daylight. I looked behind me and I could see a man walking. He started to walk towards me. I sensed he was coming. I tried shouting to some people who were sitting down in the distance. They looked like they were working as if in a class room but outside. They were all adults. As I tried to shout no sound came from my mouth. The man then ran straight past me and stopped in my pathway. He was afro-Caribbean. I stopped walking and the man started to throw glass squares at me. I knew he wanted to hurt me. I tried to move out of the way and the glass just missed me. He then came towards me and grabbed hold of me. I struggled and shouted, 'Help me, help me'. The other people started to get up but none of them came to help. I kept shouting, 'Help me' but they just walked passed.

I woke from this nightmare. I lay still, I could feel my heart beating fast and I felt an intense sadness…

Sunday, July 13th 2008

I was in an unknown house and Neil was there too. It was morning. I was looking in a mirror and my hair was all grey, 'All grey,' I said to Neil, 'Look at my hair it's grey.' It had happened over night. He said his was grey too and I told him that I might leave it and not colour it. I didn't really recognise myself.

When I woke from this dream I thought to myself, I shall just have to accept that I'm getting older. Inside I want to leave it grey. I must stop pulling out all the grey hairs, otherwise I'll have no hair left.

Thursday, August 7th 2008

I seemed to have dreamt a lot during this night.

I was dreaming I was outside with Neil and our children but somehow I had lost them all and needed to catch the train. As I walked along the road I saw my son driving his car with his girlfriend. I was aware they had both been crying. I mouthed to them that I didn't have my phone and that I couldn't find Neil. I carried on walking and came to some really steep steps; they were a red colour and made of iron. I didn't like it. I was then walking through woods; in the woods it was damp and fairly dark. I could see different people walking. It reminded me of a National Trust place. I needed to be beside the road and I was the only person walking in that direction.

I was at 56 and I'd asked my siblings to come and brush their teeth.

Monday, August 11th 2008

Flashback

I had stayed at my sister's house the night before. She had showed me the room I would be sleeping in. It was pink with dolls and teddies, a lovely girly room. We had laughed in her room as she showed me her new tilting bed. We acted silly and talked a little about our past. I had no trouble getting off to sleep. I woke at about 2.30am my heart was racing. As I turned over I was aware someone else was also in the bed. I can't describe the shock at seeing my father's face in mine as I turned over. I could smell his breath and feel it on my face. I nearly choked trying to hold the sound from my mouth. I sobbed uncontrollably, trying to make sense of it. I felt sick, frightened and alone.

The affect of this dream lasted for weeks…

Today I'm feeling sad and lonely. Neil is preoccupied but he did ask me how I was feeling. I actually didn't feel that he was that interested, just going through the motions. I asked him about his day…he said he had received an email about going to London on Thursday and Friday. I said, 'I thought you didn't need to go until after our holiday in September'.

His employers still hadn't paid back money that they owed us from a previous trip Neil had been on. I was cross and upset that

Neil still hadn't put a claim form in and that he allowed them to treat him that way. I felt he had no balls! I found him weak. I went to bed fed up and Neil slept in another room. In actual fact I love sleeping by myself as I have always hated noise at night especially the sound of breathing … even now after so many years the triggers are there in the darkness. I know we all have to breathe, but there's breathing and there's breathing.

In the morning neither of us spoke to each other, I went swimming.

When Neil returned home from work early evening he asked me if I was alright. To which I replied, 'No'. He said he hadn't liked seeing me upset and cross the night before and I asked him why. I told him that there is nothing wrong in getting upset and angry, and I still felt frustrated with him. He walked off. I felt myself getting more frustrated and angry and my tummy was churning. All I could think was, 'I really hate you'. He carried on as if nothing had happened, same old, same old… I thought to myself I'm trapped here always. I closed the back door because I could feel a slight draught. I went and sat down and then heard Neil open the back door again. Inside my head I felt impelled to shut it again and I got up and slammed the door with such force. My voice was raised and I said, 'I can't take much more of this, I need to get out'. Neil followed me up the stairs and I threw my coat at him. I shouted at him, 'Leave me alone, I don't want you anywhere near me'. Standing in our bedroom I just stood for a while, my heart was racing and my tummy churned. I wanted to scream and shout, I hated being in the house, but instead I just stood and stared. I felt I had no one and then I started to cry. I'm lonely and alone as always.

Wednesday, August 13th 2008
The dream that follows woke me in a state of panic with my heart racing and tears falling. It was 3.15 a.m.

> *I was shouting at my father to leave me alone. We were in my bedroom at 56 and he told me he was going to fuck me. My elder sister was also there. I ran into the other room shouting, asking her to help but she simply hid under the covers. Dad had hold of me, he just kept coming for me. I said to him, 'I'll stab you' and I was throwing my arms around and kicking out at him. I said to him, 'I know what you've done, you raped mum'. He replied, 'Yes'. All the others knew, but said nothing. I was frightened.*

Friday, September 19th 2008
Sent photo to the Jersey Police force via e-mail and dreamt this that night.

> *In this dream I was running away from my father. It was quite dark but I could still see. I ran up some steps and hid. I could see him, he was looking for me and he was drunk. He was close to the top of the steps and he slipped. He tumbled all the way down, rolling over and over. At the bottom of the steps in the distance I could see trees, wasteland and grass and I knew at once that he had hurt himself. I went to help him and noticed he had a cut on his head. I said to him that he needed to see a doctor at the hospital. He seemed small and I helped him up. With my arm around him I helped him up the steps. He kept*

moving his hands over my body so I told him to stop doing it. Very quietly I whispered into his ear, 'Did somebody do something to you when you were a little boy?' He looked sad and said, 'Yes'. He said he was very young and it had been a man. He kept chatting away. It was dark now and I could see 56, dad was gone. The people that lived in the next house were getting ready for a celebration and I could see tables and chairs outside. There were a few people gathering. I looked down at my clothes and thought I looked ok; I could go if I wanted to. I decided not to and walked away.

To dream of being in the dark usually represents a state of confusion or being in an unknown and difficult territory.

Monday, October 6th 2008

I was in 56 and it was dark. I was calling out for someone from downstairs. I started to climb up the stairs and it was dark. I was calling my father saying I didn't feel well. I couldn't walk properly, as if I was drunk and my vision was blurred. My father came from the bedroom on my right and started to touch me. I tried to push him away but I needed him because I didn't feel well.

I woke up.

Thursday, October 23rd 2008

Neil had forgotten something and I went to take it to him. I called him (I think it was a bus) and when I saw him his collar was up and he had no tie on. I went to straighten his collar and there was a very young woman there (a little rough looking). She was standing very close to Neil and had her head on his shoulder. She was tall and thin, with straggly hair a bit unkempt and seemed carefree. They were talking and laughing. I felt shocked. We were outside and he said he was leaving me and I told him that I could see he was happy. They were laughing and ran off and he jumped onto the swing.

I was then at home, upstairs, thinking about how old Hazel and my younger sister were and that she was going to school on her own and shouldn't be. She was about five years old. Hazel was then sitting on my left side and I had my arm around her. On my right was a little boy crying, so I put my arm around him as well to hold him closer. Down the stairs we could hear talking, it was Neil (he was the age he is now 52). Neil said he was moving in with the lady. I said to my daughter Hazel, 'Go and see what she looks like'.

I was then down stairs in another house. I had some keys which Neil had given me and the family allowance book. A lady who used to live across the road from us was also there. I was telling her how I'd stayed at home to look after the children and had only worked part time. I didn't have much of a pension and was very worried about supporting myself. I was trying hard not to cry. I was thinking I'd been so awful to Neil over the years I was glad he was happy. I felt lost but now it was too late. She asked me how I was feeling. I sat and thought and said I felt nothing, detached no emotions, just blank.

Saturday, October 25th 2008

What a messed-up night I had. I spoke to Neil before I went to bed and said I didn't understand why we were sleeping in separate rooms!

I was serving a lady who asked me for the coffee, but I didn't quite catch what she'd said. Then she said, 'It's number 23'. I said to my colleague that my tooth had chipped (2 teeth) and showed her what had broken off and she said I needed to see someone. I took the coffee to the lady but the cup was a little squashed. She asked if the coffee was hot and I replied, 'Oh yes'.

I'd arrived at a place but needed to check that no one was in. I rang the home telephone and a man answered but I didn't recognise the voice. I spoke to two other people telling them that I needed to get home because someone was in my house and taking all my stuff. I couldn't find my keys, they were broken and held together with Blu-Tack. A man came with me, it was raining and he didn't want to get wet. He was wearing a long, brown, suede coat. He fell into the car. We seemed to be going backwards down a hill. I gave way to two people on bicycles.

I was in a very old fashioned shop and it was dark outside. A man came to the door and said he had bought a dog for me to see. The dog was jumping up and I went to stroke it. I thought this was ok then realised the dog's teeth were buried in the palm of my hand. It was hurting but we managed to get them out.

I was in my sister's garden and her daughters were all there too. There were newspapers everywhere and I said they needed to be cleared away so I started to sort through them. I was climbing up some steps and it was dark. At the top of the steps there were three large plants and I needed to be very careful not to knock into them. Also at the top was a lady and she led me to a small garden. She said to the left was a garden for my sister which was neat and tidy with a beautiful, pink fuchsia in the centre. As we walked together across the lawn I picked up a yellow plant with a long thin stem, the lady remarked that it needed to be planted. I said I didn't realise it was a plant because I couldn't see any roots. She said, 'Look here, if you just plant this part it will grow'.

Dreaming of newspapers suggests knowledge that is publicly available. It may be information that we need to make sense of the world around us or it may be something which is specific to us.

Flowers in a dream usually give us the opportunity to link feelings of pleasure, beauty, development, potential and childhood.

Sunday, October 30th 2008

I was in the front bedroom at 56. Both mum and dad were in the room. Dad was in the bed and something had happened. (I thought it was strange mum saying it and not dad). Mum said to me I mustn't tell anyone about what had happened and she held both my hands. I shouted at them both and said they couldn't stop me from telling anyone, but I wouldn't say anything because I cared about them. They both looked relieved. I ran out and down the stairs. My brother was coming through the front door with some of his friends. He asked if I was ok and I said 'No'. He said nothing and went into the front room. I went into the kitchen and started to sob. The people in the kitchen just ignored me. I was standing at the sink. I saw my brother and asked him if his girlfriend was there. He said, 'No' and I continued to cry.

(On my own as always! That's how it feels at the moment in my house.)

The house usually refers to the seat of the soul. To dream of conversing with dead people is a propitious omen, signifying strength, courage and a clear conscience.

Friday, November 28th 2008

I was going down a grassy damp slope. I saw wolves coming towards me and felt very frightened and needed to get away. As they got closer they changed into men, their arms were outstretched and they were trying to grab me.

I was in a house a few doors from 56. Neil was there and we had woken up. I saw his mother and she was angry. She told us not to sleep together. I couldn't find my clothes and she stared at me. I said I'd shower at my house. We then got onto a small boat and I could hear his mother still moaning. She was saying that no one took any notice of her. There were children on the boat and I saw our youngest son. Our son said, 'Please get me off'. I then started to shout at my mother-in-law saying I can make my own decisions. Our son was calling out and I grabbed his hands and pulled him up. The boat sank. I saw people lying still at the bottom as if they were dead. I then saw black and white zebras, their stripes were maps.

Wednesday, December 10th 2008

I had some money in a money bag and it was down the front of my top. I fell over. Two people caught up with me and asked for the money but I told them I didn't have any. They shouted at me to hand it over. I replied I needed it to pay for the journey to go and see my mother. If I didn't have the money I couldn't see my mother. I started to cry.

I actually woke from this dream crying and I felt lonely and sad.

Tears in dreams can indicate an emotional release and a cleansing. Running in dreams suggest the potential for anxiety or distress, spiritually we may be trying to do something too quickly.

I was in hospital. I'd had an operation and was not allowed to get up. My chest started to bleed and weep. There were two other people there one was my sister Diane. I was wearing a really lovely pair of pyjamas but I couldn't find my dressing gown. I decided to get up and thought the pyjamas didn't need to be covered up.

I was going into a cinema to watch a film/play. I could see my elder brother with his family and my elder sister sat at the back. The seats were red velvet. I then saw another younger brother as I made my way to the front. I saw another younger sister just about to sit down and told her that I'd seen lots of members of the family and now she was here! She looked disappointed because I'd said that, it wasn't what I'd said.

Monday, December 22nd 2008

I was lying down on my right side (I had a red dress on) and Dad was shouting at me. I was getting ready for him to hit me. I could feel my body tingling. He was lying next to me and touching my body. Mandy was asleep at the bottom of the bed. I said to my sister Mandy , 'Help me, dad's touching me'. His face was close to mine and I could smell him and he started to poke his tongue into my mouth. I tried to move my face to get away.

I woke from this nightmare, upset and distraught.

Monday, January 5th 2009

Flashback and dream

Neil left for work at about 6.30 after bringing me a cup of tea in bed. I wasn't going to get up for a little while, there was no rush. I fell asleep. I heard the front door close… the nightmare begins.

> *I didn't know if I was dreaming or awake. (I had heard Neil's car so I thought I was awake. I was then aware and heard someone in the room but I thought don't be silly. I lay very still and tried peeping out of the corner of my eye. The next instance he was on top of me .... no point struggling. I felt the weight of his body and I was raped and then he was gone.*
>
> *I thought I was awake, but I must have been asleep. I woke up and it was just getting light, I then heard someone else. I was lying on the bed and couldn't move. I tried so hard to wake up but I was frozen. I opened my eyes just a little and could make out a shadow. I thought I'll just lay here (twice in one day). I thought I could hear him talking and I wanted to say something. The next thing he had hold of my legs/feet and pulled me around. He then raped me again. He seemed to be lower down this time and I put my hands out because I wanted to feel his hair. Then I'd know it was dad. He tried to move his head away but I felt it ... it was his hair, his head.*

I wake from this nightmare and feel sick oh so sick.

I don't quite know what to think, what a lonely world this is. All this in my head, I could go crazy…

Friday, January 16th 2009

> *Dreaming I was lying on my left side with my father's face right in mine. He was breathing on me licking, kissing and slobbering on my face but I couldn't move. I wanted to move my right arm and hand to move his face away but I was frozen. I wanted to call out to Neil but I couldn't as no sound would come from my mouth. I woke and it was still dark.*

I went to see Diane and we chatted about our childhoods and some intimate stuff. This was the first time I'd asked her if dad had kissed her face and slobbered on it. She said he had but it wasn't a kiss and always the same side of her face. I realised looking at my sister, at this point he had been rubbing his penis on my face and had ejaculated. God, that's just so disgusting. The realisation that the same thing had happened to her was in some respects a comfort; I wasn't mad. I wonder if other sisters have had similar experiences.

Monday, January 19th 2009

Counselling session at Choices with Helen.

I feel like I have turned a corner. I can't even begin to explain how my feelings have changed. I think because I've had the above dream for so long (dad and my face) I understand it is a message and I need to explore it. So I have asked Neil to wear aftershave when we go to bed, just so I know it's him and not my dad. It helped.

Sunday, January 24th 2009

Neil woke me with a cup of tea, he always makes me a cup of tea in the morning, well nearly always…

> *I had been dreaming of 56 again. There were problems with the gas and I was speaking to a lady on the telephone. I could hear Kevin's loud voice in the background. In a cupboard I saw flames and I asked Diane to open the doors so the warm air could heat the other rooms up. I closed the door to the hallway and was looking down at the blue carpet and dribbling. I heard dad and he was telling Diane and I off for the way we were speaking to each other, he was mocking us. I thought to myself when he pauses I'll tell him to shut up. He paused and I told him to shut up.*

Saturday, January 31st 2009

> *Neil and I were at an outdoor swimming pool. I showed my card and went to get changed. The pool wasn't busy. I called to Neil but he didn't hear me as he had already changed and was swimming. I went to find the changing rooms. I made my way down some steps and there was a rail on the left hand side. On top of the rail were some towels which I needed but I decided not to take one. The assistant came along and I asked for one, she said I could have a small towel that was ultra absorbent. I found an*

empty room at the far end and started to undress. There was a flash and I turned to look into the darkness and saw a man with a camera. Just to the right was a pile of rubbish and on top lay a small skeleton thing talking. I said, 'What's going on, what do you think you are doing?' He tried to pass me but I grabbed his legs and we both fell to the floor. His fingers were digging into my hands; I was not letting him go. I asked him why he took the photos. I shouted to another man who had come to the door to get the police. As the door opened a family were coming in to use the same room. I said to the lady and man that I needed some help. We waited for the police to arrive.

Wednesday, February 4th 2009

I woke during the night, I had been dreaming again of 56. I had woken because I needed the bathroom. I made my way in the darkness to the bathroom, passing a radiator on my right and it was hot. I made my way towards the bathroom, passing the airing cupboard on my left. I was grabbed and I couldn't get away. I called to my sister Sharon, 'Sharon help me'. I tried to scream again but no sound came from my mouth, no sound at all. I couldn't even hear my voice and I couldn't get away.

Friday, February 6th 2009

I had my own flat, front door, space and keys. I could see whoever I wanted.

There were people all around talking and getting new underwear. It was my turn to go next and I was pushed from behind. I was wearing the knickers I'd had for years. I covered my naked breasts with my arms and hands. I felt vulnerable and frightened. I wanted to tell the ladies about my abuse but another lady interrupted us. I was given a new blue pair of knickers; the ladies were laughing and saying I could have full briefs if I wanted them. I quickly made my way to the changing room (just curtains not really a changing room) and as I was getting undressed the lady came in and I was aware people could see into the room. I hated it. As she left the room she looked at my lower half.

We had moved to a new property. There was lots of work that needed to be done, it was a mess. The kitchen was large and spacious with plenty of room for a table. I said to my son, Graham, the work would take two to five years to complete. Through the window I could see the garden which was also a mess. I also saw the road through a gap which was busy with traffic. I opened the back door and was aware of the sound of the cars. I didn't understand how I could have missed that when we viewed the property. Did we view? It was too late to change now as the contracts had been exchanged. I felt sad and disappointed.

Monday, February 9th 2009

I've probably had one of the most difficult counselling sessions ever. Today I have woken up from my fantasy world. In my head I thought I could change Neil into becoming a more emotional person, who can recognise when I needed a hug, a cup of tea and someone to hear me!

But no! Wake up Denise it hasn't happened for thirty years and it's not going to happen now. He says I put up barriers, Helen clearly pointed out to me (last Friday when I went into the bedroom and he was in bed, he said 'WHAT NOW?' That's his own barrier and it shows his lack of understanding, warmth and goodness knows what else. This has upset me so much I can hardly eat. It's staring me in the face but I just haven't seen it or don't want to see it. I just don't know what is going to happen. I feel alone as always because I get nothing from him.

This probably sounds very one-sided and I don't want it to. As human beings we are very good at destroying each other, both needing something from the other person but not getting it. I'm sad and disappointed having lived in this fantasy world. I thought two people meet, love each other and grow together. There has been none of that for us, just the children. My illusions have been shattered; if there was a magic pill to make it all disappear I'd take it.

Reading the above in 2012 has made me realise just how far Neil and I have come… Learning curve for both of us.

Thursday, February 12th 2009

I was outside and inside. There were so many women around, apart from dad. He was staring at all the children, the girls. I started telling everyone without him hearing that he mustn't be left with any of the girls, not even for two minutes. Because two minutes is all it takes. I could see girls from different cultures and they were beautiful and young. One of the girls kissed my father on the cheek while he was standing in the doorway. That was all it took, he started following her everywhere. Another adult (a lady) was also there and I said to her, 'Watch him, don't let him out of your sight.' I found myself rushing from one place to another asking people if they'd seen my father. 'Where's the girl? I shouted'.

We were then outside walking up a country path and it was early afternoon. I asked some people if they'd seen him, 'Yes' they replied, 'in the woods'. He is being watched and they have radios. Another person was telling them what was happening. They were saying he is making the little girl put your mother's cloths on. I said, 'I'm calling the police, we've got two minutes. I was given a phone and I tried calling 999 but no one answered. I felt panicky and tried again. Another sister was telling me not to say anything. I couldn't understand this because what was happening was wrong. Still no answer from 999 and I said it would be too late, he would have already raped her by now. I stood waiting for the girls to come back, hurt and upset. It was just too late, oh why didn't anybody listen to me.

I was in the front bedroom at 56 with three of my sisters. The room was decorated beautifully and the bedding was lovely. The lights were new and we had an en suite bathroom tiled in blue and white. I thought how lovely it was. My sisters were all happy and we were all laughing.

The colour blue is the colour of the clear blue sky. This is the prime healing colour as it suggests relaxation, sleep and peacefulness.

Monday, March 2nd 2009

Walking along the B1000 road I was trying to get away from a lady. Her face was horrid and it kept changing. I had a pram with a baby boy inside. I was then looking through a text book with very graphic photos inside. A little boy had his head missing and was clearly dead. One leg was also missing the pictures were horrid, I didn't know what to think.

To dream of a boy shows potential for growth and new experience.

Looking out from my front door I could see an old work colleague standing and just looking at our house. I was thinking this is the first time he has come to visit me, I waited and my sister said, 'Go to him'. I waited and stood still. I watched him standing and my heart ached. He turned and I watched him walk away, he had made his choice.

How strange the mind is and playing tricks with me. My soul mate.

Thursday, March 5th 2009

I was in an unknown house in the living room. Both my parents were there. A little boy was tied up and they were going to whip him. They said the whip was very special and it was part of the ritual. I was horrified and they gave me the whip which was long and made of bamboo. I took hold of it and threw it onto the open fire. They were both distraught that I'd done that. I looked into the burning fire to watch it burn and watched the colour changed to yellow and melt into a blob. It then split into two pieces.

The colour yellow in a dream. This is the colour closest to daylight and is connected with the emotional self. The attributes are thinking, detachment and judgement.

Tuesday, March 24th 2009

I was standing in the corner of a room with cloths piled high. A little girl about five or six years old was following me everywhere. I was hurrying along, jumping, dodging things and I leapt over a concrete area. I could see planks of wood which were part covering a deep, dark, dark hole. I jumped over and the little girl followed but she wasn't able to jump over and fell in. I watched her falling, falling and there was nothing I could do to save her.

Dreaming of a child gives us access to our own inner child. We all have parts of ourselves which are still child-like and curious. When we are able to get in touch with that side of ourselves we give ourselves permission to clarify a potential for wholeness which we may not have previously recognised.

Wednesday, March 25th 2009

Neil told me they were coming, thousands of them. There was nothing we could do to stop them. As I was looking out the window I could see thousands of tiny flying things just like a swarm. They would be able to get through the cracks. I said to Neil, 'Let's go to the other end by the shower'. But there was no escape they were all flying in.

Sunday, March 29th 2009

Dreaming I was looking into a mirror and my teeth were pointing backwards into my mouth. Later I looked again and it was as if my jaw was going into my mouth. I couldn't speak, hardly at all. I walked down the stairs and my parents were sitting on the sofa. Mum on my left and dad on the right as I looked at them. I knelt down in front of them and they both looked at me. I started to tell them about my jaw and said it was time for me to go to the hospital. They both just looked at me.

Monday, April 6th 2009

I seemed to be dreaming a lot about my teeth falling out and missing teeth. I was digging a hole in the garden and burying my teeth. My next door neighbour Kim was looking over the fence.

Teeth falling out indicates we are aware of going through some form of transition, similar to that from childhood to maturity to old age and helplessness.

Sunday, April 12th 2009

Dreaming I was in 56 and moving through the rooms. In the living room two small young children appeared who were aged about four/five. I asked them if they had been hiding and if they were alone in the house. They replied 'Yes, our mother has left us she has gone away'.

I wasn't feeling too well and my elder sister Sharon was taking care of me. I couldn't get up from the chair. A man appeared and said he was looking for something. I told him he should knock first.

Thursday, April 23rd 2009

I was in the upstairs bedroom at 56, looking out of the window. A man climbed up a ladder quickly and was looking into the room at me. He was smiling. I closed the curtains because I needed to undress. I popped my head through the curtains and he said he needed picking up at seven thirty.

I drove around Welwyn Garden looking for him, when I saw him I drove onto the grass quickly to pick him up and then back onto the road. I was issued with a parking ticket and the fine was three hundred pounds. I protested that I couldn't pay the fine and it rose to seventy-five thousand.

Saturday, May 2nd 2009

I woke from this dream crying and upset. It took a few moments to become aware that I was safe and in my own bed. The dream follows…

I could her people arguing, I'm not sure if it was 56 or not. There were older and younger siblings around. Both my parents were in front of me and they were standing. I was younger than I am now. They told me they had never wanted me and had hated me from the moment I was born. I was so upset and couldn't understand what had I done. I could also see my husband and he didn't want me either. I felt so alone. I saw people from previous jobs and I tried to explain to them what had happened. I just wanted them to listen to me. I saw a lady who I'd worked with a few years ago and she gave me four pens. The pens were shaped like fishes, two were silver and two a bluish colour. I placed them in between the covers of a book and started to close it. The lady said to me, 'How long are you going to keep mine?' I said, 'Sorry,' and gave two back to her.

I was thinking to myself, I needed a job, I was quite distraught. I didn't know where to go. I was then in an upstairs room. I could see that the room was sparse, just a few tables and chairs. On the table I could see business cards and telephones. Someone said we have a job for you, selling overcoats to companies and that they had already sold a few. I noticed a man who I knew, he hugged me. I said to him that I loved him, he just held me.

This is not the first time I've dreamt about overcoats!! I need to explore it.

Saturday, May 9th 2009

In this dream I'd been out shopping for clothes and had bought a few items for my brothers and sisters. Back at 56 the house was busy with people, mum, dad and the children. Mum was curled up, lying on the settee. She started to speak but I could only understand part of what she was saying. She said she had also been shopping. (Because she hardly ever spoke, it was so lovely to hear her voice and I was overwhelmed). I asked her what she had bought. She had three bags with her and she took a long white skirt out of one and gave it to one of my younger sisters. She then gave something to someone else, I don't remember who. Lastly she gave me a bag. Inside was a white blouse which was made of thin material, like polyester. There were three buttons down the front and it was short sleeved. I thought to myself I'll never wear this, it's not my style. I thanked her for it and told her that I'd wear it.

When I woke from this dream I kept thinking how lovely it was just to hear my mother's voice. It made me feel happy all day.

When numbers are drawn to our attention in dreams they can have either a personal or a symbolic significance.

a) Your ideas for stability and success will materialise.

b) Freedom, bravery, fun, enthusiasm, brilliance, listlessness, over-confidence, impatience, lackadaisical behaviour.
c) The triangle, freedom.

White. This colour contains within it all colours. It suggests innocence, spiritual purity and wisdom.

Sunday, May 17th 2009

In my old bedroom at 56, I had a bag full of old baby clothes and a few ladies' tops. A little boy about one year old was on the bed crying. There were different toys on the bed, cars, tractor etc and I put a few toys into my bag. A lady came into the room and went to take one of the tops and I said to her that she couldn't have the pink one. I had paid five pounds for the bag and she looked surprised. I was waiting for someone to come and take the little boy.

Another little boy was crying upstairs.

Tuesday, May 26th 2009

I had gone to visit my elder sister. In the middle of the floor there was a cat tray and I asked her if she'd got a kitten. She replied 'Yes'. I looked to my right and saw a new puppy with long floppy ears and sad eyes. As I looked further into the room I saw a little boy. I asked my sister how old he was and she said seven. I asked her if she was fostering him and she replied, 'Yes'. I could hear another sound and the little boy was peeing into a potty.

Friday, June 12th 2009

I was standing next to a well/hole. Aunty Lily stood next to me and was holding onto a rope which was attached to a heavy object. It was far too heavy for me and I let go, it fell into the deep well. I shouted at Lily to let go but she held on and was pulled down into dirty water. I couldn't reach her, I tried so hard to reach her. She was just to far away (down). She had no way of climbing out and there were no side grips. There was no escape. Lily lay on her back in the water and started to drown. She was taking great big gulps of air and water. Lily stopped moving, she was lifeless and blue.

I woke from this dream feeling incredibly sad. I miss my Aunty Lily (mum's sister).

Saturday, June 13th 2009

I am at an unknown house with my eldest son who was about ten years old. Looking out of the front window I see a white car pull up outside with two men inside. I was aware they were trying to find a way into our house. I ran around frantically closing all the windows and checking the doors. It was dark inside the house. I could hear one of the men speaking to a lady. Suddenly I heard a knock at the front door and the back door at the same time.

I thought how stupid do they think I am. I'm not going to answer one so the other person can come in the other door. I kept very quiet and still. I crouched down, I could see them looking through the window. The man was telling the lady to dig the putty out from the window frames and then they would be able to get in.

Wednesday, June 17th 2009

This was not a dream.

At work today my boss had spoken to me about wearing a

uniform, which made me feel sick and panicky. I could not have predicted my response and explained to her exactly how I felt. We spoke a little about the counselling I was receiving and she was lovely to me. I spoke to both my bosses at length about my father and my past home life; this was something I had never been able to do at work. So for me it was a huge relief to be able to tell them even if I did get upset, I hope they understand.

I dreamt that night…

> *I was sleeping in a bed and could hear my father shouting. I got up to listen and knew he was in one of the other rooms. I knocked on my elder brother's door and asked him if he could hear the shouting, he replied, 'Yes'. He got dressed and we made our way to the front door. There were other family members there also waiting. My elder brother went in front of me to take the lead. I whispered that I'd heard my father say he wanted to kill us, 'Yes,' my brother replied, 'That's why I'm going first'.*

Thursday, July 16th 2009

> *I was to get into a lift at the hospital. The lift was outside a concrete building. There was a work colleague with me, a nurse. I was holding my youngest son in my arms and then he was walking at my side and holding my hand. In his other hand he held some reins which were attached to a horse. It was damp, dull and overcast and in the distance I could see undergrowth and trees. I was doing my best to try and get back to the lift. I saw barbed wire and we kept getting*

stuck in the wire fence. The horse then became tangled in the fence and had to lie down. I could see the horse's teeth and it wasn't breathing properly. My son was still attached to the horse by handcuffs and was suspended in the air with his arms outstretched. I was trying to cut his clothes to free him. There was a man and I called to him to contact the emergency services. Another man came through a door on my right and I shouted at him to do the same.
Later I saw the horse in a field looking as if nothing had happened.

I decided to lie in bed for a while this morning, something I very rarely do. I'd had my early morning cuppa and was relaxed. Neil went off to work, the front door closes…

I drifted off to sleep … I felt someone rush into the room. I knew at once he had come, the covers moved slightly. I fought with myself to wake up; I did not want this…

I woke up!
So, I tell myself – it will still happen even after all this time – will it ever go away – probably not?

Monday, July 20th 2009
Today I've had my counselling session, Helen has looked through some writing that I'd started and given it back to me today. I have been thinking about it on and off. Helen says I need to write a lot more about myself and today I value her thoughts and comments. I'm glad I gave it to her, I have so much to do and because I'm going through my healing process

and it's so very difficult I have decided to take a break from it. Having kept diaries for so long I have all the information I need to continue at a later date.

I dreamt my son-in-law Ali had made a robot out of rubbish with a dustpan for a mouth. It was talking and moving around. We were all saying how good it was and how clever Ali was for making it.

Saturday, August 1st 2009

Have had a horrid evening with Neil just talking about stuff we usually talk about.

I dreamt I was lost, upset and I was telling a man in the street that I'd been on holiday. We had moved but I couldn't remember where I lived and I was crying. I tried to climb up a muddy slope but I didn't know where I was going.

To experience ourselves as being lost denotes confusion on whatever level is depicted in the dream. It may be emotionally or mentally as much as physically. It shows we have lost the ability to make decisions.

Saturday, January 30th 2010

We had run out of heating oil in the cottage and it was freezing. I had taken myself to bed because I was so cold and knew I'd be warmer there even though it was only five-thirty in the afternoon. I was thinking about 56 and being cold there so many times, this must have been a major trigger.

This is what I dreamt…

> *I dreamt I was in my cold bedroom at 56. I had woken up and sitting on the bed was a young girl of about six or seven years old. She was naked. I looked down at her tiny body and at her vagina – naked with no hair. On her left inner thigh I could see a large round bruise, I just thought she had been raped.*

When I woke up I kept thinking about her (me). Bloody 56 again, it will haunt me forever.

* * * * *

Today is new, the past is dead.

Monday, May 24th 2010

Today is my final counselling session with Helen. As I look back since my first session on 8th October 2007 I think how quickly the time has passed. This morning I read once again what I had written on that day, all my fears and hopes. I wrote about my sadness and I cried on the way home with Neil beside me. I said to him I don't know what will happen. I dreamt that night and woke the following morning exhausted, sad, detached and with a thumping headache.

But today, two and a half years on, I feel different. Yes, I have butterflies in my tummy and I know my journey is not yet complete. As I continue to change and accept that there will be days when I feel sad, lonely and lost I shall remember I have my close family to support me and of course my books. I feel quite tearful, thinking about how Helen and I have worked together and how she has supported me unconditionally throughout this life-changing time. I am forever thankful to her for being a part of my jigsaw.

Helen gave me a card with a picture of a lily and inside she wrote the following words:

Dear Denise
I salute your courage
Working with you has been
A joy and I'll always think of you
With love and admiration
Best wishes
Helen

Monday, October 24th 2011

I dreamt this dream before I was woken up by Neil with a cup of tea at 07.20 a.m.

> *The dream was in black and white. In a house there were lots of people waiting to use the bathroom. Dad was in front of me and he was very small. The shower curtain kept moving down the rail and I was only half dressed. I was running, trying to get home. I needed a shower before school. The time was just before 08.00 a.m. It was raining and I could see lots of my siblings. I thought we needed to go straight on but one of my siblings said no it's right. She had read the bus.*

I was then in a house standing on a chair and looking through dusty old books and other papers on the top shelf of an old dark wooden unit. I found a book containing some school work, a poem I had written. There was also a letter written by (Lawrence) about mum not being well. I could see other members of the family and some were also looking through some stuff. I was thinking how lucky I was that I had this information. My elder brother had put a record, a 78, onto the turntable. It was a voice but not my father's, that of another man. My brother said it was dad's story but someone else was saying it. It started off by saying it was 1957, then telling us about when my elder sister was born, then 1958 when my brother was born. (Sounds just like my book)

I could see my sister Sandra sitting on a chair and to her right was a younger brother. He was pushing his hand under her arm and then into her hand to hold. She turned to her left and took hold of another brother's hand. Not far from where she was sitting an older sister sat, I beckoned to Sandra to get the brother to hold her hand too and they were all joined together.

I woke from this and felt moved and sad. If Neil hadn't have come into the room who knows what I might have seen.

As I sit here writing this I understand the message I am getting, my thoughts are we will always be joined together as a family even if we are apart. Writing the book and giving it for all to receive. OUR STORY!

Another dream early morning, Friday, October 4th 2011
Dreamt in black and white again. There were photos of my family when we were children. An old case with letters and cards. A poem written by my father and in the left corner the words that say 'I wonder if anyone will read this?' Also a small card with writing about a girl who was born but didn't live long. It appears it was abroad somewhere not in the UK. Two other sisters sitting together speaking about their abuse and writing things down. Four other ladies all discussing that the abuse was untrue.

Many of the dreams, flash backs and nightmares that I have, have an intensity of emotion which I do not feel at any other time. During this dream state the need for me is to run or get away. This usually happens just before submission. I have read that this is because it would be too painful to get into that submission state. The dreams and nightmares that I experience appear to arise from the following causes.

a. *Childhood fears*, perhaps also centred around the same situation, though the fears at this stage also include the fear of being attacked and anxiety about one's internal drive. This may be to do with the child's need for survival and satisfaction of basic needs of food, warmth and shelter. (It has been noted that if these needs are not satisfied the child withdraws into a world of its own. If therefore the rage it experiences is suppressed this could surface later in nightmares.)

b. *Childhood memories of intense emotions*. These are often centred around loss and it has been suggested that such dreams are to do with the birth process and the attendant trauma.

c. *Post Traumatic Stress Syndrome*, where again the basic need for survival is threatened. It has been found that the anxiety experienced can still surface a after a long period of time. Some people are still experiencing such nightmares many years after the event or events.

The affect and effects of my abuse are with me every single day. There is nowhere to hide. Most days in my world I am sad but I choose not to show it, although I am sure it shows through. People say I am a strong person and yet inside I am in pieces forever. Nothing can or will take the pain away. It is part of me. I still try to understand what makes a person behave in such a dysfunctional way. I have also heard people say 'You will get over it'. To me it is clear that they have never been abused, sexually, mentally, verbally…

CHAPTER TWENTY-THREE

A Little About Me

Me and exercise

I have always exercised with a passion; I love the feel good factor it brings and the adrenalin rush. I remember my father telling my mother she was fat and I thought I don't ever want to be overweight. In my early years the weekly walks with my younger siblings were a ritual. I loved to run at school and ran cross country for the school – I never lost. I was chosen for the school hockey team and didn't always play with the stick because the teacher said 'I didn't need it', my feet did a good job. I played badminton, took step classes in the eighties as well as joining the gym. I always made time for exercise.

Another passion of mine is swimming and I always swim at least twice a week, sometimes three. Usually at 7.30 a.m. I feel its appropriate to say a big thank you to Elaine (life guard) from Biggleswade swimming pool for always noticing how I'm feeling and asking how's the book is going.

I have also been practising Hatha yoga for four years and this has helped me enormously both physically and spiritually. Most people think that yoga is just about poses and strange positions but it isn't. Yoga is a whole system of physical, mental and breathing exercises and for me gives a sense of wellbeing and peace. My yoga instructor Les Gray is brilliant and his classes are always challenging, informative, fun and I know for sure that when I'm ninety I'll still be able to tie my own laces.

The meditations during yoga are very powerful and during

one I was transported back in time and felt strong emotions that had been buried. Memories of when I was a little girl, vulnerable and lost. I also felt a strong sense of inner calm and strength.

I made a commitment to my healing process some years ago. For me new challenges, risks, fears and opportunities are all part of my healing.

I have read The Empty Mirror by James Lincoln Collier and this book only highlights my frustrations. I am sad when I think the answers to life are so simple, yet most people just don't get it! Today, I feel alone in my thinking and wonder if perhaps I am slightly mad. As a child I lived in a world of disassociation and detachment, very similar to a deep meditation. How strange I should choose to put myself into this very place. Reading The Empty Mirror invited me into a world where I feel I have already been and I'm drawn towards it. However, the contrast between a Buddhist life and a western life are so different and I need to find the right balance between the two.

If someone were to ask what other interests I have, I would reply 'I have many. Pre-Raphaelite Art, travelling, Paganism to name but a few. Give me a pair of hiking boots, a rucksack and I'll walk for miles in the rain or sunshine. If I'm outdoors I'm at peace. Spending time in my garden is pure bliss and I can potter all day in the overgrown, wild flower beds. There is always something new to discover in between the weeds. I know it's probably really boring to some but I love it.

A New Start

Over the years I had attended different courses to try and better myself, but I always found them hard, because I always doubted myself and my ability to pass the exams. I had passed all my exams at school but I'm still not sure how. My education continued – I took courses in computing, counselling, customer care and then a Practitioner's course in NLP. This I found to be most helpful. I learned new things about myself and it gave me the courage, belief and motivation to take a diploma in Life Coaching. I set up my own business and practised until the start of my counselling in Cambridge. The Life Coaching took a back seat while I dealt with my own skeletons that had been hiding for so long. The two and a half years that followed were the most difficult of my entire life.

Now in 2012 I am ready to pick up where I left off. The scene is set, my office is ready, and I welcome new clients to coach.

Bringing Back Memories

Over the years I have often passed 150 and thought about knocking on the door, so one sunny morning in 2012 I decided to do just that. This particular day I felt different somehow and made the journey with a slight churning in my stomach. I drove past familiar landmarks such as St Mary's church where I was baptised and later married, down the big dipper, a road that dipped like a fairground ride and up the other side passing my first school, Harwood Hill on the left. The doctor's surgery on the right (thoughts of mum, the GP notes flashing through my mind), the local shops just on the left, then a slow snail's pace as I stop outside 150 on my left.

I feel a little nervous as I park my car, but being a good yogi I take a few deep breaths and feel instantly calmer. I don't remember getting out my car but I'm making my way down the steps, the only real difference is a concreted parking area, otherwise it is much the same. As I knock on the door, time stands still, and I touch a cold metal pole that holds the roof cover over the front door. Once again I was a little girl, standing, waiting to be let in. No one answered the door – this was not what I'd planned at all. I had imagined I would be let in by whoever now owned the house, I would skip from room to room and I would feel; well I'm not quite sure what! Maybe some deep trapped feelings from long ago.

There was only one thing to do and that was to knock on the neighbour's door and ask what time the residents of 150 would be home; if they knew of course. You can imagine my surprise when it was answered by an elderly lady who I sort of recognised. I explained about being born in the house next door and she asked if I was an Arm, to which I replied, 'Yes'. I politely asked, trying to hide my excitement at the same time, if she would spend ten minutes of her time telling me about my parents. She agreed and I followed her in.

Once inside her house we were joined by her husband, who had been in the garden, and we sat for a while chatting about my family. They both confirmed that my mother was indeed unwell and that she would swing from being happy to very depressed, constantly up and down they said. They had moved in to their house at the same time as my parents in 1957/58 and it was lovely to see this couple still living in the same place.

It made me think that my parents could still have been alive and living in the same house. 'Don't be ridiculous Denise, wake up' a little voice echoes in my head. I looked around the room and imagined a mirror image of the house next door. I longed to go and look inside, but today it was not meant to be, that would have to wait until another day.

They gave me little snippets of information that are invaluable and I am so glad I came. They confirmed that my father was a bully to my mother (*their words not mine*). They told a little story about my father putting up a fence post in the garden and losing his temper because he couldn't get it in the ground. Apparently he had hit it so hard he damaged a recently planted pear tree and to this day it grows at an angle into the neighbour's garden.

They also told me that, for my parents to qualify for a council house in Welwyn, my father would have needed to work in Welwyn for at least two years. He worked for a company called Rank Bush Murphy, which I understand was involved in entertainment, radios etc. I had no idea about this job of his and have no further information as this would have been before I was born.

After we moved from 150 to 56 my mother on odd occasions would telephone the couple to keep in touch. I was surprised to hear that but a little piece of the jigsaw puzzle none the less.

I would like to say a big thank you to Albert and Joan, it was lovely to see you both again after so many years and looking remarkably well.

That part of my journey completed I made my way to 56 just to see how the place had altered over the years. As before, I drove the familiar route from Knightsfield to Haldens, just a five minute drive in the car. Passing by the local shops, I realise the buildings are just the same but the shops are different. I turn right into Sloansway and up the hill with the Mayflower pub on my right and as I look right I see Timbercroft. As I pass houses that still look the same I feel nervous and have a sense of someone watching me, which seems to cloud my normal rational thoughts. The turning now is just ahead, left into post fields. Thoughts of school friends pop into my mind which takes me back almost thirty-five years. Then straight ahead stands number 56 and I drive slowly towards it. I'm caught between my life now and my life then. Part of me wants to knock on the door, part of me says, 'It's nearly over'. I drive closer, slower and come to a gentle stop. I'm half expecting my father to come out, with a cigarette in one hand and whisky in the other. My breathing is faster now, I don't hear crying, though I'm crying, crying for all the lost years. I'm weeping for the loss of innocence. My tummy is tight and there is a lump in my throat that is choking me. Where is my mother, where are my brothers and sisters? How can I find them, I need to protect and comfort them. The house stands cold, lifeless, an empty soul before me. I am for this moment in time, stuck in the mirror, The Empty Mirror. I hear the voice in my head, 'That was my life! Was my life. Yes Denise that was your life.' I need to drive away, away from this oppressive, dark, haunting space. I start my car and slowly drive past heading to the A1 that takes me HOME.

On the return journey home I play my music and sing, I sing so loud to Simply Red as the tears fall freely behind my dark glasses. 'As I look into your eyes I see the sunrise, the light behind your face helps me realise.' I love my husband more than words can ever say. He has loved me unconditionally and until now I did not know what true love was. Today I do.

When I arrive back at home, for the first time I see things differently, I park my car on our small gravel drive. I sit for just a brief moment and pinch myself; this is my home, a real home for the first time and I am safe. I make my way through the arched Iron Gate and ring the bell that hangs to the left. The ringing echoes in the still air. My eyes are drawn to the trees and carefully planted hanging baskets which are now in full bloom. Our cottage garden is wild with flowers that have self-seeded and made their home wherever they choose. I love it just like that. The seventeenth-century thatched cottage takes pride of place and every day my heart skips a beat at the sheer joy of living in such an idyllic place. This was my dream from long ago as I lay on the grass behind 56, dreaming and staring at the skylarks in the clear blue sky. I have always had hope in my heart, because without hope there is nothing.

Hope is the thing with feathers
That perches in the soul....
And sings the tune without words
And never stops....at all

I close the front door, the picture is almost perfect. I see my children, my husband, my life and my chocolate box cottage. I am at last at peace.

September 24th 2012
Today I'm meeting Helen my ex-counsellor to catch up after no contact for nearly two years.

Visit Eric in the village, catch up on the previous week's news and run the vacuum around for him. I am very fond of Eric Blott; he is the father figure I never had. A gentleman in his eighties and full of the most marvellous stories. We laugh together, he makes me a cup of tea, and I pretend he is my dad…

Yoga tonight at 7.30.

Justice given, lesson learned; I receive what I have earned

Life goes on…

From Neil my husband, my best friend and my soul mate.

'Invariably I struggle to find the right words to express myself. I just seem to get tongue-tied, and what words do come out are often (with hindsight) inappropriate. Denise has invited me to write a small contribution for this book and yet again I'm struggling. Potentially I could write a parallel volume that would be wrong because this is Denise's story of her life through her eyes. It is a diary of survival, an investigation into the past and search for the truth. 'Yes, these things happened' and I am sure more pieces of the jigsaw will appear in years to come.

I can remember a counsellor saying to me that abuse is not really a topic of everyday conversation. 'It is not something that you talk about,' she said. Decades have passed but the articles you read about in the newspapers today are actually the tip of a huge iceberg. Abuse, whatever its form, is devastating for the victim. However, it is like a stone thrown into a pond: ripples spread out and affect others, whether they are other family members, partners or friends. If you are one of these other people I urge you to acknowledge the truth. Denial is as devastating and destructive as the abuse. I strongly recommend you read *Allies in Healing* by Laura Davies. It certainly helped me enormously, and above all I believe.

I keep saying to Denise that this book is one hell of an achievement. However, she is dismissive of this, but I have watched her write this from the start. I cried when I read the last page, I'm crying now.'

References

10,000 Dreams Interpreted, Pamela Bull, 1998

Meditations For Women Who Do Too Much, Anne Wilson Schaef, 1990

The Stone Child, Dan Poblocki, 1990

Women Who Run With The Wolves, Clarissa Pinkola Estes, 1992

The Road Less Travelled, M. Scott Peck, 1990

All photographs are from the author's own collection.